SELECTION
SUCCESS!

SELECTION SUCCESS!

HOW CONSULTANTS, CONTRACTORS, AND OTHER PROFESSIONALS CAN INCREASE THEIR SUCCESS IN A QUALIFICATIONS-BASED SELECTION PROCESS

LORI STANLEY
HILARI WEINSTEIN

Mill City Press
Minneapolis, MN

Mill City Press, Inc.
212 3rd Avenue North, Suite 570
Minneapolis, MN 55401
612.455.2294
www.millcitypublishing.com

ISBN - 978-1-934937-31-0
ISBN - 1-934937-31-2
LCCN - 2008937939

Cover Design and formatted by Sophie Chi

Printed in the United States of America

CONTENTS

INTRODUCTION

ou've been selected!" That's what firms want to hear after they've committed significant time, energy, money, and resources to create a Statement of Qualifications submittal and prepare an interview presentation for a public works or private sector project. And this is what firms will hear more frequently when they provide the right information in a way that allows the owner to give the firm the most points possible in a selection process.

Although this book is generally written to address consultant and contractor selections for public works projects, this information is also applicable to many private sector selection processes. It is created to assist participants in a selection submittal and interview process, whether it is the firm's principal, business development director, marketing coordinator, project manager, or the technical project team. In short, this book will be invaluable to anyone participating in public or private qualifications-based selection (QBS) processes.

The QBS process is becoming more and more common in both the public and private sector. It is frequently used by owners in order to choose consultants and contractors based on the proposing firm's capabilities and project understanding rather than a competitive low bid process. Consultants and contractors interested in working with public agencies or private sector owners must be able to successfully participate in this selection method to be considered competitive by these important clients.

The QBS process may be based solely on a Statement of Qualifications (SOQ) submittal that interested firms prepare and provide to the owner in response to the owner's advertisement. Owners may, however, use the SOQ as a tool to shortlist firms and invite a limited number of best qualified firms to participate in selection interviews.

In the SOQs and in those interviews, the selection panel will get a lot of information from firms they consider to be qualified. How can YOU stand out? How can you differentiate yourself from the competition? How can you demonstrate to the owner that you are the right selection?

In most cases, owners have a choice of competent firms to provide the professional services they require. The question, then, is what can *you* do to improve your firm's chances in getting selected for the project you've targeted?

This book is not designed to offer a step by step process for developing your SOQ and interview presentation. Each client is different and each project is unique. Nor is it meant to be a replacement for the assistance of a skilled consultant who specializes in preparing teams to interview more effectively. This book *does* provide valuable tips, tools, and ideas to help improve your SOQ and interview processes.

Preparing a rater-friendly SOQ and enhancing presentation skills will help your firm be more effective and engaging, and result in winning more projects. You will stand out from the competition, and your team members will feel better about their individual contributions and have more confidence in future presentations.

Who better to provide these tips than Lori Stanley of Selection Solutions Consulting and Hilari Weinstein of High Impact Communication!

Prior to creating her consulting company, Lori supervised the Contracts Administration Section for the City of Phoenix, Arizona for almost 18 years. She was responsible for managing consultant and contractor selection processes for projects citywide with construction values ranging from $500,000 to $1 billion. In that position, Lori read and rated thousands of consultant and contractor SOQs and managed hundreds of interview processes. This has allowed her the unique opportunity to witness the best (and the worst) that firms have provided to the owner. With her experience, Lori understands what is needed and appreciated by selection panel members.

Over the last two decades, Hilari Weinstein has been involved in speaking, sales training and presentation coaching. An inspiring and talented coach, she has worked with numerous firms throughout the U.S. to make their interview presentations more effective and engaging. In addition to serving on the faculty for the American Council of Engineering Companies Leadership in Engineering Administration Program, she is a contributing writer for *Southwest Contractor* magazine.

Lori and Hilari come at this subject from different perspectives. But collaboratively they offer something that has never before been available in book form to those who work in architecture, engineering, consulting, and construction. No other book offers all these valuable, industry-specific tips and ideas which can make a significant difference in a qualifications-based selection process. Enhancing submittal documents and presentation skills will help your firm increase your chances of Selection Success!

SECTION I

FOUNDATIONS

◆

*"Today's preparation determines
tomorrow's achievement."*

Unknown

CHAPTER 1

BASIC TERMS

I n this book, we will be using some terms that are generally standard in the industry. However, we recognize that some owners may use variations on these terms. In order to make sure that we are all on the same page, below are our definitions.

Qualifications-Based Selection Process (QBS)

A qualifications-based selection process is any selection process that bases the consultant or contractor selection on specific criteria that are non-price related. These criteria can be standardized and applicable for most processes; however each process can also include criteria that address specific needs of that proposed project. These could include:

- Firm experience on similar projects
- Experience of key team members
- Project understanding
- Amount of current work with the owner
- Principal office location, home office for key team members, and/or use of local resources
- Public relations/public involvement expertise
- Ability to provide detailed cost estimating on incomplete plans
- Complex program management experience

As mentioned in the introduction, the QBS process may be based on a Statement of Qualifications submittal that interested firms prepare and provide to the owner in response to the owner's advertisement. The owner may also require an interview presentation from the firms as part of their selection process. As long as price is not part of the selection criteria, this is considered a "one-step process".

There are also variations on the QBS process that can include a price component for consideration. In this "two-step process", owners will shortlist firms on qualifications (which may include an interview), then require the shortlisted firms to provide a cost proposal for some or all of the required services. The cost information is then factored into the final selection.

Request for Qualifications (RFQ)

The Request for Qualifications is a document frequently prepared by the owner and used in the project advertisement process to:

- Describe the project
- Describe the services to be provided by the selected firm
- Describe the selection process to be used
- Identify the selection criteria
- Provide submittal requirement information
- Provide other owner rules and regulations
- Identify an owner contact person.

Owners may also refer to this document under various titles including Request for Proposal (RFP), Request for Letter of Interest, or may choose to include this basic information in their project advertisement.

Statement of Qualifications (SOQ)

Firms interested in competing for the project are requested to submit a Statement of Qualifications that addresses the selection criteria provided by the owner. This Statement of Qualifications document is sometimes also identified as a Proposal, Letter of Interest, or Qualifications Submittal.

Shortlist

Shortlisting is the process used by owners to select which firms will be invited to participate in the next step of the selection process (i.e. interviews, site visit, cost proposal).

In order to identify the best qualified firms, owners will review all the Statements of Qualifications received. The selection panel will review the SOQs and meet to determine which firms to invite to the next step. Firms reaching this next step in the selection process are considered to be "on the shortlist" or "shortlisted".

Project Interview

A project interview is a presentation to the owner's selection panel. The format and time allotted varies by client, but will likely include a combination of a prepared presentation by the firm and/or questions from the panel.

Now that we all have a mutual understanding of some terms that will be used frequently throughout this book, let's move on to your first step toward Selection Success.

CHAPTER 2

GOING FOR THE JOB

"If at first you don't succeed…try, try again." Good advice? Well, sometimes yes, and sometimes no. Good business development managers know that success often requires submitting a Statement of Qualifications (SOQ) on numerous projects to an owner before your firm will get selected. They also realize that you can't submit only on projects where you are absolutely confident that you are the best qualified. Firms have a number of factors to consider when evaluating whether to compete for an advertised project.

This is not an exact science. On one hand, we all know that it takes a significant commitment of time and resources to prepare a good SOQ and occasionally firms have to make choices regarding which advertised projects they should pursue. On the other hand, other firms that have more comparable experience might not be selected for some reason (too much current work with the owner, they don't have their "A" team available, they submitted a poor SOQ, etc.). Sometimes you might submit on the right project at the right time where being "well qualified" is good enough to beat firms with more direct experience.

It is understood that firms will frequently target particular owners/agencies as part of the upcoming year's marketing plan. Firms then closely watch that owner for opportunities to submit their qualifications for projects being advertised. Submitting multiple SOQs to one owner on a number of different projects gives the various owner representatives an opportunity to become familiar with your firm name, your qualifications, and your team experience, which is not a bad thing…..*as long as you are a reasonable candidate for each project.* **Do not submit on any projects for which you are not well qualified!** Not only is preparing an SOQ time consuming, but you never want panel members to read your document and ask themselves "Why did they waste their money and my time submitting on this project?!"

How do you decide whether to submit or pass on a project? And if it's a "go", how do you increase your chances of getting selected? The following are some basic elements that will start you on the path to a successful submittal.

1. **Determine whether you are really qualified for the project.**

Firms that are well qualified:

- Have successfully provided similar services on comparable projects.

- Will offer a team where members have good experience providing the required services on comparable projects.

- Can provide documented references to validate the team members' capabilities and project successes.

- Have a good understanding of the project scope and its issues, and can provide creative and effective solutions to mitigate the specific project's unique challenges.

- Will demonstrate that their firm can provide all the resources required for this project.

In addition to being qualified, an owner wants to know that this project truly matters to you and will receive a significant amount of attention and enthusiasm from your firm. If you are a larger firm that has worked on multiple projects for that owner, you'll want to emphasize the importance of maintaining your successful working relationship. If you are a smaller firm or a firm new to that owner, you'll want to emphasize the importance of this project to your firm and your strong desire to create a new and lasting working relationship with this client.

2. **Attend the pre-submittal conference.**

    If you have decided that you are interested in competing for the project, determine whether there is a pre-submittal conference and if it is mandatory to attend in order to submit a SOQ for the project. Whether mandatory or not, your marketing person and key project team members are strongly encouraged to attend because:

    - It is the best way to hear from the owner's team what the project will entail and what issues are anticipated.

    - You can ask questions to the owner and can hear questions from other firms that are attending.

    - You'll find out who your potential competition is.

    - You can identify firms that might be potential teaming partners.

    - It shows the owner that you are interested in the project.

3. **Identify the right team.**

    It is imperative that you gather a team that demonstrates the experience and project understanding necessary to deliver a successful project to the owner.

    - The Project Manager is one of the most important members of the team and, at best, should be able to show significant project management experience on similar projects. Your Project Manager should show either significant project management experience on somewhat-similar projects or significant experience in another key role (Project Designer, Superintendent) on very similar projects. If your Project Manager cannot show good comparable experience, *either find another Project Manager or consider passing on the project.*

• The Project Manager should play an active role in leading the team from SOQ creation through construction completion. Owners value continuity in the primary point of contact on the design and construction teams. They also want someone throughout the project duration who understands not only *what* decisions were made but *why* those decisions were made during the design phase in order to address project questions intelligently during construction.

• Any organization chart included in your SOQ or interview should clearly show the key team members and should identify both design phase team and construction phase team members. It should also be easy to see what team members are involved both in the design and construction phases to show continuity of the team.

The next two pages provide examples of a Consultant and a Construction Manager at Risk (CM@Risk) organization chart that provide required information in an easily understandable format.

Sample Consultant Organization Chart

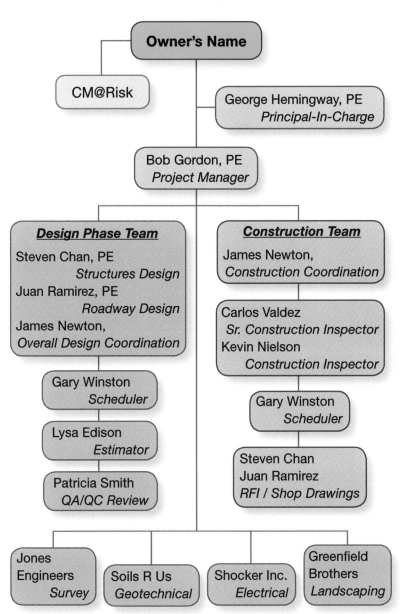

Sample CM@Risk Organization Chart

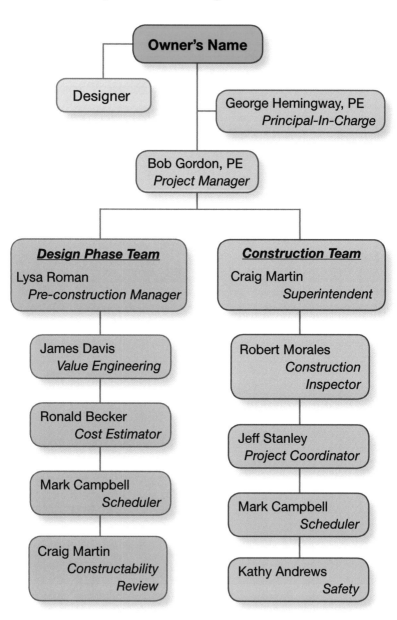

4. **Read the advertisement and/or Request for Qualifications (RFQ) and follow the SOQ requirements.**

Identify and be sure to comply with the requirements identified in the advertisement and/or Request for Qualifications, including:

- Statement of Qualifications (SOQ) submittal page limits. Verify:

    - What is included in the page limit (i.e. organization chart, references) and what is in addition to the page limit (i.e. resumes, professional certifications).

    - Whether an introductory cover letter is allowed and if there is a page limit.

    - Whether the SOQ cover, the Table of Contents, or section dividers are counted as submittal pages.

    - Whether there is a page size requirement (8.5" x 11" vs. 11" x 17") or any font size or margin requirements.

- Number of submittal copies to be provided. Also verify the required format of submittals (i.e. bound, unbound, electronic copies).

- SOQ due date and time. Do not cut this too close… traffic congestion or accidents can delay travel to the submittal location, so plan for extra driving time. If a firm is depending on mailing or delivery service, plan to have the submittal package arrive at least one day early.

- SOQ submittal deposit location.

- Any specific documents or information that must be included in addition to the SOQ responses (i.e. special certifications, affirmative action documentation, acknowledgement of addenda, etc.).

Following the SOQ requirements is the most important step a firm can do in a qualifications-based selection process. Regardless how perfect you may be for a project, if you're disqualified for not following one of the SOQ requirements, you're out!

If you can put the right team together and if you prepare a powerful Statement of Qualifications following the owner's requirements, you are heading down the right path to Selection Success.

NOTES

KEY IDEAS IN THIS CHAPTER:

_____

_____

_____

_____

_____

_____

ACTION ITEMS:

_____

_____

_____

_____

_____

_____

CHAPTER 3

GENERAL COMMITTEE INFLUENCES

The selection panel has significant responsibility in the selection process. They should be knowledgeable about specific project requirements, be prepared to read the submitted material and meet when required, and should have an open mind that will result in a fair selection of the most qualified firm. However, it is unrealistic to believe that the panel members' personal experiences, preferences, and opinions could be completely separated from their selection recommendations.

Why do firms want to consider who will be on the panel? Identifying prospective panel members will help firms to tailor their message to meet the needs of the committee and to address specific project elements.

Most owners will not release the names of the selection panel members. However consultants or contractors interested in submitting on a project can frequently figure out at least some of the potential selection committee members. Depending on the owner/agency, the panel will frequently include:

- Project Manager
- Contract Officer
- Project User Representative(s) (if applicable)
- Funding Department/Client Department Representative(s)
- Designer
- Contractor Representative

So what does that panel need to know about you?

- What prior project experience does your firm have that is applicable to this project?
- What prior project experiences do the team members have that is applicable?
- How much does the selection panel already know about your firm and your team?
- Does your team understand the panel members' specific "hot buttons"?
  - ◆ Schedule
  - ◆ Budget
  - ◆ Minimum firm supervision required
  - ◆ Acceptance of owner's contract
  - ◆ Willingness to start work prior to contract finalization

- ◆ Facility maintenance
- ◆ Minimized inventory requirements
- ◆ Community coordination
- ◆ Project site safety
- ◆ Security

All "hot button" issues should be addressed in the discussion of project understanding in your SOQ and interview.

- Why should they hire you for this project?

  - ◆ What do you know about this specific project?
  - ◆ How will you make their life easier?
  - ◆ What expertise do you have that will increase the likelihood of project success?

There's another thing to consider if you are a contractor interested in submitting on a Construction Manager at Risk or Design/Build selection process: Why do owners want to use this alternate delivery process on their project rather that using the traditional design-bid-build selection method?

- They can confidently select a contractor who can successfully complete the project and meet their needs, rather than depending on which firm submitted the lowest bid.

- It allows contractor involvement during the design phase to assist in design recommendations and constructability reviews.

- Owners always know where they stand on budget and schedule.

- It provides improved budget control and allows owners to make necessary scope changes during the design phase rather than waiting until the project is bid.

- If money is still available toward end of construction, owners can add wish list items to the project or get excess money back.

- It avoids bid day surprises.

- It simplifies the option for phased construction.

- It allows for early purchase of long-lead items.

- It encourages good performance by the contractor if they want to be selected again.

- Overall, it generally makes the owner's life easier.

Demonstrating in your SOQ and interview that you understand their needs and will bring these benefits to the project will make you a stronger competitor.

In summary, catering your message to the owners' concerns in both your SOQ and interview will improve your chances of being selected for the project.

NOTES

KEY IDEAS IN THIS CHAPTER:

_____

_____

_____

_____

_____

_____

ACTION ITEMS:

_____

_____

_____

_____

_____

_____

SECTION II

THE STATEMENT OF QUALIFICATIONS

◆

"You have to learn the rules of the game.
And then you have to play better
than anyone else."

Albert Einstein

CHAPTER 4

PREPARING POWERFUL
SOQ CONTENT

Your message matters! Your message must be on-target. It should lead the selection panel to the conclusion that *your* team is the best fit to meet *their* needs on *this* project.

Your Statement of Qualifications (SOQ) is your firm's introduction to the selection panel. This is the first, and possibly your only opportunity to deliver your message to the project decision makers. Providing the right information in an easily understandable format will make both your SOQ and your interview more successful. Therefore, let's start with some ideas to make your SOQ content more effective and memorable so you can get to the interview shortlist.

As you start preparing your **Statement of Qualifications** keep the following hints in mind:

1. **Gather the team**

   Preparing a successful SOQ must be a joint process that includes your marketing/business development person in addition to the key project team members. Although your marketing person can provide the preliminary and final format of the document, it is the project team members who will provide project understanding, identify the key issues, and explain how they should be addressed. By providing project-specific information in your SOQ rather than a generic submittal with standard boilerplate language, you will demonstrate that you have taken the time to study the project and that your team is best qualified to provide the services required.

2. **Read the SOQ criteria in detail**

   What information is the owner asking for?

   - Past project information (description, cost, date completed, firm's/staff's role on project)?
   - Major project challenges and project approach?
   - Examples of documents?

   Make sure that you completely read each question and answer all parts of the question.

   In her selection process, Lori frequently included the following question:

"Describe the challenges and concerns your team has identified on this project and explain your approach in dealing with these issues. Of all the issues, identify the three most critical challenges that must be addressed." This was deliberately written as a broad, open question that would allow firms to really impress the panel about what they knew about the project and how they were going to address possible issues. This question had one of the highest point values in the selection process.

This question has two specific parts looking at two very different components. The first part asks firms to discuss everything that you know about this project and the issues that you will need to address. For this, you should provide lists of project issues. Even though you probably won't be able to discuss every item at length, you can list ten to fifteen items and address five of them in more detail.

The second part of this question asks for the top three issues that you will be addressing on this project. This part of the question is looking for your opinion of prioritizing the importance of the project issues. This is a very different thing from the first part. The most important things on a project may be (but is not always!) the project construction budget or a tight project schedule. But it might also be coordination with the surrounding community; it may be the complications of building a project in an active site; it may be trying to meet the requirements of various different user groups. It's important that you consider the project carefully and make this response project specific.

The overall question is pretty clear, however firms that did not really read it closely would frequently answer this question by saying "You asked us to address three issues on this project......" and would only talk about three items! These firms lost a lot of points and frequently lost the project by not reading the question closely and answering all parts of the question completely.

3. Format your SOQ according to the criteria provided

There are two good reasons for this:

- It's a good way to make sure that you have addressed each item in each question.
- It makes it easier for the selection panel to know what question you are answering and what information what they should be looking for.

Both of these items will help you receive the most points possible from the selection panel.

4. Provide relevant firm or team experience

The experience of your firm is an important consideration when owners decide who to select for their project. It gives the selection panel confidence that the firm has previously been successful in providing the services that will be required on the project being advertised.

However, even more important, is the experience of the specific team members that you are assigning to this job. *In fact, the two most important selection criteria are usually the experience of team members and understanding of the project* (which will be discussed in item 6).

A discussion of the firm or team's experience should include the following:

- *A good description of the project* – just giving the project title doesn't give the panel the information it needs to score appropriately.

- *The construction value of the project*, if applicable – was it $200,000 or $2 million or $10 million? The panel needs to know how your project compares in size to theirs.

- *Dates of the project* (either duration of the study/ design or of the construction) – was the project done one year ago or ten years ago. It makes a difference.

- *Role of the firm* (prime or subconsultant) or role of the team member (project manager, project designer, superintendent, etc.). Do not assume that the selection panel member will read any attached resumes. Firms must provide the required information within the pages allowed for the SOQ.

- *Relevant personnel* – which team members on this new project were involved on the project being discussed? While it's nice to know that the firm has some comparable experience, what really matters is the experience of the personnel being proposed for the new project. The panel will also consider whether these team members have experience working together.

- *Your project is comparable because*….. – firms shouldn't assume that the interview panelists will automatically understand how the project experience being discussed is comparable to their project. This is especially important if you are not showing projects that are the same (i.e. a park for a park, a library for a library). Make sure that you list the reasons why your experience on each previous project will make your team stronger on the new one. Comparable items can include:

  - similar services provided (design, construction administration, CM@Risk, etc.)
  - similar project scope
  - previous experience with this client
  - accelerated schedule
  - working on an active site

It is important that you provide all this information on team experience in the body of your SOQ. You are being rated on what you provide within the pages allotted for your SOQ. Do not just refer the reader to the attached resumes!

Below is a sample of a project description for the "Firm Experience" section. As you see, this provides all required information in an easily readable format, is attractive (using picture and colors), and emphasizes why this is comparable to the new project.

Smith Library – City of Phoenix, Arizona

 Masters Architecture Inc. was selected as the prime architect to provide programming, design, and construction administration services for this 30,000 square foot public library. The facility included adult and children sections, a rare book room requiring special HVAC and light control systems, state-of-the-art computer and electronic systems, and a public community meeting room with complete audio-visual capabilities. This library was completed within the original project budget and schedule.

Comparable because:
- Branch library
- City of Phoenix project
- CM@Risk project
- Public involvement
- Complex HVAC
- Same key team members

Const. Budget: $5.8 million
Final Const. Cost: $5.78 million
Const. Completed: April 2007
Contact Persons:
    Linda Houston (602) 555-1212
    Robyn Skrams (602) 555-1215

Relevant Personnel:
    Lisa Rudnicki – Proj. Mgr.
    Bryan Summers – Proj. Arch.
    Tim Stanley – Struct. Eng.
    Candace Gormley – Mech. Eng.

---

5. Use a matrix

The more information you can provide regarding your team's experience, the greater your chances will be to get selected. We realize that firms are generally limited to the space they have to provide this important information and it can be difficult to demonstrate the full scope of your team's experience. However, that information must be easily understandable. A matrix is a very useful tool to get a lot of key information in a small space.

As you see in the following examples, there are a variety of formats that you can use to demonstrate your team's experience.

PROJECT NAME	FIRM ROLE	RELEVANT PERSON	ROLE	COST	YEAR
Phoenix 91st Ave. WWTP	Prime	R. Smith T. Stanley	PM Des. Eng.	$30M	2007
Phoenix 23rd Ave. WWTP	Prime	R. Smith T. Stanley	PM Des. Eng.	$15M	2006
Scottsdale Water Campus	Prime	T. Stanley M. Jones	Des. Eng. Elect. Eng.	$10M	2004
Glendale WWTP	Prime	R. Smith M. Jones	PM Elect. Eng	$22M	2005
Mesa WWTP	Mech. Sub	J. Jackson	Mech. Eng	$10M	2006
Tempe WWTP	Elect. Sub	M. Jones	Elect. Eng.	$18M	2005

This first example above is for a wastewater treatment plant project. You will see that its primary focus is on the firm's comparable project experience. However, not only does it show useful information regarding the various projects, but it also provides important project personnel information. This matrix is particularly effective when used at the end of the Firm's Experience section. After describing three to five comparable projects in significant detail, use this matrix to showcase many more comparable projects in a relatively small space.

Name/ Project Role	Registration	Years of Experience	City of Phx Experience	Public Agency Projects	WTPs / WWTPs	Pump Stations	Pipelines	Reservoirs
Elizabeth White, Principal	AZ PE	30	●	●	●	●	●	●
Travis Stanley, Project Mgr.	AZ PE	28	●	●	●	●	●	●
Kathy Crosby, Project Eng.	AZ PE	5	●	●	●	●	●	●
Jose Martinez, Structural Eng.	AZ PE	28	●	●	●	●		●
Tim Rudnicki, I & C	AZ PE	30	●	●	●	●		
Matt Villa, Resident Eng.	AZ PE	16		●	●	●	●	●
Ron Beal, Sr. Inspector	ICBO	10	●	●	●		●	●
Ana Summers, Inspector	ACI	18	●	●	●	●	●	●

The second example shown above provides significant information for the "Personnel Experience" section of the SOQ. As you see in this example, the top of the matrix identifies specific personnel information and general project experience (owner, project type). However, you also have the option to identify various project titles along the top and indicate how your team has experience working together. Again, this is best used in addition to a detailed description of key project personnel experience.

This final example below is a matrix that easily shows both the team members' experience on comparable projects (in this case roadway projects) but also demonstrates that this team has significant experience working together.

Experience Matrix	Highline Blvd. $12.2 m 2007	48th Street $9.9 m 2006	Robson Bridge $23 m 2006	Madison Ave. $7.6 m 2005	Jackson Pkwy. $13.8 m 2005
R. Smith, PE, Project Mgr.	●	●	●	●	●
M. Cherno, PE, Project Eng	●	●	●		●
R. Sosnowsky, PE, Structural Engineer	●	●	●		●
G. Goodridge, PE, Roadway Engineer		●	●	●	●
J. Rudnicki, PE, Traffic Engineer	●	●		●	●
N. Summers, PE Hydrologist	●	●	●		
D. Washchuck, PE Quality Control	●	●	●	●	●

6. <u>**Show detailed project understanding**</u>

As mentioned earlier, the project understanding section is generally one of the two most important sections of an SOQ. When addressing a question regarding the scope, challenges, and issues that can be expected on a project, show the owner that you know what they know on the project and more!

- Make it project specific – show that you've been to the site. For example:
    - site issues – soil challenges, drainage, washes, material laydown space
    - environmental issues – project view corridors, solar impact, shading, green material usage
    - neighborhood issues – safety, security, noise control, dust control
    - street issues – traffic control, dirt tracking

- Identify issues that they might not have thought about and show that you know how to address them.

This is the one area where every team has the ability to impress the panel with their project-specific knowledge. This section requires significant involvement by all team members to identify detailed issues and provide well-considered solutions. Determine for yourself how much effort you wish to expend on this section, but know that firms that put in the extra effort here significantly increase their chance of selection success.

7. **Resumes**

First, it's important to understand that many, if not most, panel members do not read resumes. But just in case, make sure that your resume is both useful and follows the SOQ guidelines.

Most resumes show education information, professional registrations and a list of the person's project experience. Here are some other resume suggestions:

- Check for page limits on resumes.

- Modify your resumes for each submittal to include relevant projects only….do not show a laundry list of unrelated projects.

- For each project listed, include the role of the firm or person and project construction value, if applicable.

- Some owners are specific about what they will allow in resumes. Make sure that your resumes do not include non-appropriate information (general firm information, project pictures, etc.). These items may be considered firm experience which might result in that resume page being counted toward the maximum number of SOQ pages, causing you to exceed allowable pages. If you have questions, check with the owner's contact person regarding the legality of information included.

8. **Other general suggestions**

- Notify each person named as a reference that they may be contacted and verify their current contact information.

- Be accurate! If, while checking references, the client finds your information to be incorrect or false, it diminishes your credibility and can have a negative impact on your ability to get selected for this or any future project with this client.

- **Judicious bolding is good**. Too much is not good (it is a strain on readers' eyes over a long period of time). To make it easy on the readers, bold key issues, highly comparable items, and information you do not want them to miss.

- Use reasonable type size (not less than 10 font). If a selection panelist has difficulty reading a firm's SOQ, they are much more likely to skim over it and give fewer points.

- Use bindings or folders, not corner staples. It sends a more professional message.

- Be careful with boilerplates. If a rater is working on a City of Phoenix process, they don't particularly appreciate reading, "We are looking forward to working with the City of Scottsdale on this project."

- Avoid pages and pages of text. Pictures, graphs, and matrices will make the SOQ much more attractive, interesting, and easier to read and comprehend.

- Make your submittal neat – make sure that there are no typos, watch bullet indentations, and use appropriate page breaks (avoid single line "widows" and "orphans" when you paginate). A sloppy SOQ speaks to your firm's poor quality control.

Now that you know what it takes to prepare powerful SOQ content, you're ready to start preparing for the interview process.

<u>NOTES</u>

KEY IDEAS IN THIS CHAPTER:

_____

_____

_____

_____

_____

_____

ACTION ITEMS:

_____

_____

_____

_____

_____

_____

SECTION III

THE INTERVIEW PROCESS

◆

"To be persuasive, you need to make a good first impression by establishing trust through attitude (body language, voice tone) and personal packaging; you have to present your case with indisputable logic; and you have to give a tug to the emotions."

Nicholas Boothman

CHAPTER 5

THE IMPACT OF THE INTERVIEW PROCESS

F ew things cause more panic in an architect, engineer, or contractor faster than these two words: Interview Presentation.

Your firm has been shortlisted which means that you have shown your team to be technically capable. The interview gives you the opportunity to sell your team and their ability to manage critical components of the project.

Having worked with Interview teams for many years, we have heard our share of disaster stories and creative excuses to avoid being in interviews. One fellow would get so nervous that he'd break out into a profuse sweat, soaking his shirt during interviews. In another case, right before the interview started, the Project Manager turned green, headed toward the nearest men's room, and left the rest of the team to go on without him. Then there was an estimator who seemed to have an amazing number of family illnesses coincide with interviews.

Presenting has, for many, become a necessary evil in the consultant and construction business. It is also a critical skill that must be developed for two reasons. First, it is a process frequently used by owners to select firms for their projects. You need to be able to interview to get work. And second, in that process, your team represents your organization. It is vital that your team members project a positive image.

People in this business love to design or build projects. They aren't necessarily natural presenters. When your personnel are unskilled, uncomfortable, or unprepared, they are more likely to send a negative impression to the selection panel that could cause you to lose the project.

How do you avoid making costly mistakes?

1. **Find ways to make interviewing enjoyable.** Every team knows dollars are on the line. This adds stress and pressure, so try to make presentation preparation as positive and enjoyable as possible.

2. **Let your team know you appreciate their efforts and value them.** When we are appreciated and valued, we are more likely to put in the extra effort and go the extra mile that may be necessary for success.

3. **Give them the skills and tools that will help them do a good job.** You wouldn't send someone into the field without the skills and tools necessary to do their job. Yet many firms fail to provide their people with the skills and tools necessary to help them skillfully interview. Frequently, firms look to their business development staff to create the presentation and help coach the speakers. And some of these business development personnel are very capable of providing this guidance. However, while they may be great at marketing and may have public speaking experience, coaching presenters requires a unique skill set that some may or may not have. Additionally, some team members may be more willing to take direction from an outside expert. If in doubt, consider hiring an experienced presentation coach, where you are likely to see dramatic results in a short period of time.

Fortunately, interviewing is a skill that can be developed by anyone if they are willing to invest the time and effort to become more effective. The good news is that this does not have to be a difficult process.

Most of us talk about work-related projects with colleagues and clients every day. We effortlessly discuss issues, challenges, and how we address them. And yet, when it comes time to interview, panic sets in because each presenter wants to do his or her best, especially when a big project is on the line.

An interview presentation should feel to the presenter like a structured, professional conversation. This discussion should lead the panel to conclude that your firm is the best fit for *their* needs on *this* project. It is your team's response to the question, "Why should we hire you for this project?"

How your team members present themselves tells the panel much about your firm. What do *your* interviews say about your company? Do you seem prepared? Do you appear to have interest and enthusiasm in the project? Does your appearance and demeanor suggest respect for the process and the panel?

Getting on the shortlist means you are qualified. But then so are all the other firms that have been invited to present. Interviews offer the selection committee something the SOQ can't provide – an opportunity to hear from, interact with, and have a conversation with your team. The interview helps the panel get a feel for <u>who</u> they might work with.

The effectiveness of any communication is influenced by both the message as well as the messenger(s). While both will have an impact on whether or not you are selected, many firms spend a majority of their interview preparation time just outlining the message leaving limited time to rehearse.

If a team gets just a couple of run-throughs before the team goes to the interview they are setting themselves up for disaster. One person may go off on a tangent that takes the team off track. Another team member might be unable to articulate his thoughts, becoming so uncomfortable and nervous that he doesn't seem like himself. The unfortunate result – the panel doesn't hear the intended message and they don't really get to meet your team.

Remember, over the course of many hours, your panel will be hearing a lot of information from several well-qualified firms. Therefore, both the content and the delivery need to be highly memorable. To stand out, the message has to be powerful and your team members must get the message across in a way that is effective and engaging.

But does the messenger *really* matter?

Hilari was leading a workshop for a large construction firm and posed the following question: Let's say you are interviewing two prospective project managers: John and Marcus. Both have the experience and qualifications you are looking for. Both are creative problem solvers. Both could get the job done. In your opinion they are equally qualified. You have one spot. Who gets it? What makes the difference? One estimator responded, "When all things are equal, I'd pick the one I like best, the one I *want* to work with. The one I like and trust more."

BINGO!

We all want to work with people we like and trust and your panel is no different. So beyond the words, how can you help the panel *feel* you are the right choice?

Exhibit the 7 C's:

1. **Confidence** – Winning teams have tremendous self assurance in their capabilities without appearing arrogant. There is a visible pride in the company they represent.

2. **Competence** – Have you really done your homework? Do you know what *really* matters to this client on *this* job? Have you taken the time to understand the important features of the project? Have you come up with creative solutions to potential challenges?

3. **Credibility** – Relevant experience on comparable projects illustrates that a firm is capable of managing the critical elements of the job.

4. **Caring** – Winning firms appear team-oriented, hard-working, passionate and proud of the work they do. They seem genuinely interested in being part of this project, as well as working with the owner and stakeholders to make it a success.

5. **Connection** – Hilari conducted an in-house training program for a national architectural firm. At the beginning of the session, the CEO posed this rhetorical question: "What do clients tell us is the primary reason

we don't get selected? We just didn't connect." His team nodded in agreement. Are you truly connecting with the panel?

6. A **Conversational** Tone – We are not suggesting that your team aim to be polished, flawless presenters. They should however, appear natural and comfortable speaking. The panel should get the sense that the person speaking before them is the same person they will be talking to out in the field.

7. **Chemistry** – Does your team have it? Do they seem like cohesive unit that works well together?

Now that you understand the impact of the interview process, let's look at how the selection panel is influenced.

<u>NOTES</u>

KEY IDEAS IN THIS CHAPTER:

_____

_____

_____

_____

_____

_____

ACTION ITEMS:

_____

_____

_____

_____

_____

_____

CHAPTER 6

HOW THE SELECTION PANEL IS INFLUENCED

As the poet laureate Maya Angelou once said, "People will forget what you said, people will forget what you did, but people will never forget how you made them feel."

By being more engaging, your selection panel, your clients and your peers will remember MORE of what you said, MORE of what you did, and they will remember YOU more favorably – increasing the likelihood of your being selected.

Think about any major decision you have made: a house, a car, a job, a spouse. Why did you make that choice? Are all purchases made because the option selected is the most affordable and practical? Or are there other elements that can influence our decisions?

Psychological research suggests that we make decisions first based on feeling, then justify it based on logic. Your selection panel is no different. It is important to understand that people are influenced by what they hear, what they see, as well as what they feel. Often what we feel shades what we see and hear.

We are not suggesting that delivery can make up for not knowing the project. Nor are we suggesting that every member of your presentation team have the polish of a professional speaker. That would actually diminish credibility of certain team members.

What we *are* suggesting is that exclusively focusing efforts on developing the presentation content and visual components such as boards and PowerPoint can be short-sighted and will likely result in failure to secure the project win. *How* your team delivers the message *does* affect what the panel members retain, how they interpret the content, and the impressions left in their minds.

Here are some of the things that are seen, heard and felt by the selection panel in the interview process.

What is seen?
    Stance
    Walk
    Posture
    Body language

Eye contact
Grooming
Dress
Visual aids

What is heard?
Clarity
Persuasiveness
Knowledge
Content
Project approach
Competence
Credibility

What is felt, sensed, or perceived?
Confidence
Connection
Team chemistry
Sincerity
Passion
Attitude
Ability to listen
Pride in your firm

Now that you have a better understanding of the three ways your audience is influenced, it is time to prepare powerful presentation content that will demonstrate credibility and competence.

NOTES

KEY IDEAS IN THIS CHAPTER:

_____

_____

_____

_____

_____

_____

ACTION ITEMS:

_____

_____

_____

_____

_____

_____

CHAPTER 7

PREPARING INTERVIEW CONTENT

The time to begin thinking about interview strategy is while you are preparing the SOQ. And, ideally, interview preparation should begin shortly after you have submitted the SOQ to the owner. We recognize this may not always be realistic on every project. However, if you know the client has a tendency to offer a short window of time between notification and interview, waiting until the shortlist comes out might not provide sufficient time to thoroughly prepare for the interview.

Make it easier for the selection committee to say "Yes" to your team by following these recommendations:

1. **Do your homework.**

    Similar to SOQ preparation, it is critical in the interview process that the presentation team demonstrate a clear understanding of what it will take to design or build the project, and what issues matter to the owner.

The following items will enable your team to speak passionately and intelligently to the questions posed in the formal presentation as well as Q & A.

- Know the project

- Know your audience

- Know what matters to the client and their key concerns

- Know what makes you the best fit to meet their needs on this project. While you may have a good relationship and significant experience with the client, several of your competitors may as well. Identify what makes your firm particularly well qualified.

2. **Make content creation collaborative.**
   First, we know that it can be a challenge to pull the presentation team off of projects in order to prepare for presentations. We also recognize that there are presentation organizers who have more of a dictatorial approach to planning content. They plan it out, create the PowerPoint, and tell each participant what to say. While the intent is to make it easier for people working on other projects, collaboration between marketing staff and project personnel will make your presentation much more effective. Each participant can provide a different and valuable perspective. As the team begins taking ownership in the presentation and their role in it,

they'll create that team energy that is critical to making the interview flow. Increase the likelihood of success by making your presentation development process collaborative.

3. **Never assume that the panel:**
   - Knows you or remembers what was written in your SOQ. It may have been months or years since they last worked with you. It may have been weeks since they read your SOQ along with 20 other submittals. You have to address every question as though you are brand new to them...because you probably will be new to at least one voting member of the panel.

   - Can remember all of your team members' names and their roles. Make sure that you introduce your full team.

   - Knows the acronyms you use. If a presenter uses an acronym that is not familiar to a panel member, that panel member may focus on trying to figure out what the acronym means, potentially missing the next portion of your presentation.

   - Knows when you move from one point to another.

   - Has industry knowledge.

4. **Answer the questions as asked.**
   Make it obvious to the panel which question you are addressing by:

- Summarizing the question at the top of the slide or presentation board.

Question #1 - Experience of the Firm

Smith Library – City of Phoenix, Arizona

Masters Architecture Inc. was selected as the prime architect to provide programming, design, and construction administration services for this 45,000 square foot public library. The facility included adult and children sections, a rare book room requiring special HVAC and light control systems, state-of-the-art computer and electronic systems, and a public community meeting room with complete audio-visual capabilities.

Const. Budget: $5.8 million
Final Const. Cost: $5.78 million
Const. Completed: April 2007

Relevant Personnel:
  Lisa Rudnicki – Project Manager
  Bryan Summers – Project Architect
  Timothy Stanley – Structural Engineer
  Candace Gormley – Mechanical Engineer

Comparable because:
- Branch library
- City of Phoenix project
- CM@Risk project
- Public involvement
- Complex HVAC
- Same key team members
- Same key subconsultants
- Provided full programming, design and construction administration services
- Project completed within original project budget and schedule

When you rehearse and present, we recommend restating the question. This will help the panel follow along as you move from one question to the next (or one part of a question to the next part). For example: "In the second part of Question #1, you asked us to identify our team's experience on comparable projects." If you change the order for any reason, you will need to explain that to the selection committee so they can follow along. Otherwise they might get lost and you might lose points.

In most interview processes that Lori managed, the first interview question was "Discuss the experience of your specific team members in projects of similar scope and complexity. Describe your team members' role in the projects identified, the project construction cost and the project date."

This question was included for two reasons. First, this will remind the panel (who may have last read the firm's SOQ three weeks earlier) why they invited this team to the interview in the first place. Second, this allows the panel to score the individual team members' experience in the interview (which is frequently one of the highest point value questions in the interview process).

Imagine how surprised one of Lori's interview panels was when one firm said, "We have limited time for this presentation. Since our experience was included in our SOQ, we are going to skip Question #1 and go right to Question #2". At that point the firm could have basically packed up and returned to their office because they just received a big zero for Question #1. You can be sure that when a firm receives a zero on one of the interview questions, it's very unlikely that they will be selected for the project!

5. **Make your answers powerful, memorable and effective by supporting your answers with relevant project examples and testimonials.**

- Project Examples
Have your marketing team keep project files for each job your firm has completed. The project summary should include:
  - ◆ the project team
  - ◆ project features
  - ◆ project challenges and how you mitigated those challenges
  - ◆ estimated and actual budgets
  - ◆ estimated and actual schedule
  - ◆ team members
  - ◆ photos that illustrate features, critical elements, completed work, a ribbon cutting and a few smiling faces.

- Testimonials
Testimonials are a wonderful way to let others brag about you and illustrate your value to previous owners and stakeholders. Marketing and business development professionals should create files by client and also by subject.

  Those subjects might include: schedule, budget, Construction Manager at Risk, Design-Build, partnering with a particular firm, and value-engineering. Start collecting these on every project.

Tips for getting testimonials:

♦ Ask!

♦ Testimonials do not have to be long

Make it easy for them. How?

❑ If in a conversation, they say something that would make a terrific testimonial, right then and there say, "Wow. That means a lot. If I were to type that up and email it to you, would you put that on your letterhead so we can share it with prospective clients?"

❑ If you have done a particularly good job for them on any of the subjects listed above, ask them to jot down a couple of sentences that describe what you did for them. For example, "Joe, you mentioned that you have been really pleased with the creative and efficient ways we have been able to manage your schedule. Might you be willing to write a couple of sentences that could help others understand what we were able to do for you?"

6. **Demonstrate a track record of success on comparable projects.**
This will build credibility and confidence that by selecting your team, they are likely to have similar project success.

61

7. **Highlight key elements of the SOQ; in particular, the key differentiators between you and the competition.**
   Since it has been a while since they reviewed your SOQ, it is wise to touch on what makes your team unique. What can you offer? What are they getting by selecting your team and how will you add value to the project?

8. **Help them get to know your people.**
   Give them something the SOQ can't – an opportunity to get to know, like, and trust the people that make up your team. These are the people they may be working with during the project's duration. One simple way to do that is by planning how these individuals will be introduced during the interview.

   Most people have difficulty talking about themselves so let others do the bragging. The Principal or Area Manager should introduce the Project Manager. Then have your Project Manager introduce his team. These introductions should be more than name, title, how long they have been in the business, and project responsibilities. Help the panel get to know the people behind the titles. What unique characteristics does each team member possess? Keep it simple, personal, and memorable: "Jeff is organized and detail–oriented. Owners love Rachel's commitment to taking care of all stakeholders. I know I can count on Marco to do whatever it takes to get the job done right."

9. **Get to the point with brevity.**
   Some folks have a tendency to just ramble on and on and get sidetracked. That can be very dangerous in an interview presentation. You're only allowed a limited amount of time and you have so much knowledge to share.

   Many architectural, engineering, and contracting professionals have to be very detail-oriented to do what they do. Yet a presentation is like going on vacation. You have this whole closet full of clothing and one suitcase. You can certainly try to cram lots of things in there but, in reality, you should only take the items you are really going to need.

   In interviews, it's important to be selective about what you're going to say, and that's why practice is so important. With practice, you are more likely to identify what is really important, you will be consistent in your message, and you will keep your timing appropriate.

   Why does this matter? It's important because going too long could adversely affect your team's ability to address all the issues you wanted to discuss. Let's say you've been provided a letter from the owner that identifies specific questions to address during your interview presentation. The first speaker's question is worth 10 points and he goes over by two minutes; the second speaker's question is worth 15 points, he goes over by three minutes; and the third speaker's question's worth 15 points, and she goes over by another two minutes. The last speaker, whose 20 point question is worth the highest point value, is now short seven minutes. How are you going to win? You probably won't. So out of respect for the panel and out of respect for your peers, when you practice, time every single run through because speakers cannot afford to go over their allotted time.

10. **Provide your team ample time to prepare and rehearse.**

It can be hard to get your team members off their other projects to prepare for the interview. They have responsibilities. Yet, when your folks are uncomfortable and unprepared in an interview, they are more likely to make costly mistakes that could send a negative impression to the selection panel. Get them covered on the job site. No excuses. Limit cell phone use during presentation preparation sessions. Have a few scheduled breaks so participants can respond to calls.

11. **Make the most out of your presentation team's preliminary content strategy session.**

- If you are going after a public project, the owner often provides a shortlist notification letter with a series of questions to be answered. Make sure that every member of the presentation team gets a copy of the letter and the SOQ. Both should be reviewed prior to the preliminary team strategy session.

- If the owner does not provide specific interview questions, your team should identify key areas to address during your presentation based on:

  - Your understanding of the project.

  - Your understanding of owner concerns.

  - The "hot buttons" of your anticipated selection panelists.

  - Project challenges your team has identified.

  - The strengths that your team brings to the project.

- At the preliminary strategy session, review the questions posed on the shortlist letter. **Read them out loud to ensure accuracy and avoid misreading the question.**

- How much time do you have to present? If questions were provided, identify an approximate response time per question based on the point value of each question.

- Determine what sort of visual elements are permitted (i.e. PowerPoint, boards.)

- Find out what the interview space will be like. This is critical. *If possible, visit the room* to do two things:

◆ Diagram the room so you can set up the practice space to resemble the presentation space. There are all sorts of stories of teams that brought boards, and then found there was really no place to put them except in front of the projection screen. Or of teams getting thrown because the set-up of the interview room was different from how they rehearsed and their planned seating arrangement no longer works. Diagram the room!

◆ Test acoustics and sound. Some of your presenters are louder or quieter than others. You have worked too hard on the presentation to have someone completely muffled by the air conditioning unit in the presentation space. Presenters need to be aware that they may need to adjust volume to be pleasantly heard.

• Discuss potential panel members. Identify their hot buttons. What might matter to them individually?

For example: The Director of Engineering, Lou, is a bottom-line, numbers guy. Budget is his issue. What can you do to give him peace of mind regarding your ability to work within a budget and perhaps save him money? Joe is a new Project Manager for the department and while you don't know him well, one of his hot buttons is likely to look good for his new boss. What can you do that will make him look like a genius?

66

- Collaboratively and directly outline the best answer to each question posed and pack a punch by:

  - **Providing a power statement** – For example: "We are the Valley's GAC Treatment Plant Specialists."

  - **Supporting your response through illustrations, examples, testimonials** – For example: "In the past 4 years we have designed 4 of the last 5 projects comparable to yours including XYZ."

  - **Expressing "What's in it for them" (WIIFT)** – Translate a feature or a strength of your organization into a benefit for this owner on this project. For example: "We understand that the City is on a tight schedule. This is a proven team with the experience and expertise critical to delivering the City a constructible design within 12 months."

12. **Determine what visual elements will help the panel better understand your responses.**
    Visual aids can be effective tools to help convey your message. These visual aids might include an organization chart, PowerPoint slides, proposed schedule, photos, charts, site maps, or structural drawings. How you use these tools can impact the success of your presentation.

It is now time to develop those highly effective visual complements to your presentation which will improve your chances of Selection Success.

<u>NOTES</u>

KEY IDEAS IN THIS CHAPTER:

_____

_____

_____

_____

_____

_____

ACTION ITEMS:

_____

_____

_____

_____

_____

_____

CHAPTER 8

VISUAL AIDS

Visual aids are speaker support tools. All too often, interview teams use them as a crutch to mask poor presentation skills. However, when used properly, visual aids enhance the message and allow your presenters be as effective as possible.

Remember that the interview offers something the Statement of Qualifications cannot provide: face time to interact with your team. Therefore, it is important to *minimize* the amount of time the panel's focus is directed to slides or boards and *maximize* the time they are visually connected to your presenters.

The following tips will assist you to optimize visual components whether they are on presentation boards or PowerPoint slides:

1. Maintain template uniformity throughout the presentation.

71

2. Keep it simple.

3. Consider incorporating owner, designer and contractor logos. If appropriate and clean, include these on the opening and ending slides.

4. Use pictures of comparable projects – particularly elements that will be required on this job.

5. Use photos or aerials of the proposed project you are interviewing for.

6. If using bullet points, it is best to have no more than 6 lines and use no more than 6 words per line. The words should prompt discussion by the presenters. **The slides should not be the script.**

7. Ideally, limit words and use images and graphics to tell the story because people remember pictures more than words.

8. Indicate the question being responded to. For example:
   1a. Team and experience
   1b. Comparable CM@Risk Projects

9. Have a light background with dark writing on your presentation slides. It is much easier for the panel to read.

Interview Agenda

- Introduction
- Experience of the Firm
- Experience of the Team Members
- Project Schedule
- Project Issues
- Closing Remarks

The following are some things that you should avoid on your slides and boards:

1. Too many words. Simplify text by focusing on ideas rather than sentences

2. Junked up slides. Slides that have too many pictures or graphics makes comprehension more difficult for the panel. Less really is more.

3. Using confusing charts or graphics that detract from the message. Sometimes charts and graphs are necessary, but explain them well.

4. Too many slides. You don't want to give the panel whiplash with slides changing every 30 seconds. Ideally, you should spend at least 45 to 60 seconds per slide.

5. Busy slide backgrounds. As in the sample below, they make it very hard for the panel to read your presentation information.

6. Dark slides

Lori has two absolutely true stories that demonstrate the disadvantages of dark slides.

In the first example, Lori managed an interview process that was held in an interior interview room that had no windows and where the lights were either very bright or completely off – there was no dimmer switch. One firm used a PowerPoint presentation that had a dark gold background and soft white print.

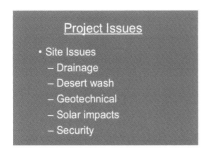

The presenters quickly discovered that the bright lights in the room washed out the slide lettering making the slides completely unreadable. However, if the lights were turned off in the room, the dark gold background made the room very, very dark and the panel couldn't see the presenter in the front of the room......they only heard a "voice in the dark" speaking from somewhere in the front of the room.

To make matters worse, because the room was so dark, the presenter realized that he couldn't read the notes he had prepared for each slide. Finally, as a last resort, the presenter had to stand in the doorway behind the selection panel to read his presentation notes by the lights in the hallway! Not too surprisingly, the firm was not selected for the project.

In the second example, one of the firms had a distinct advantage going into the interviews. As it turned out, that firm used a PowerPoint presentation that consisted of slide after slide of black backgrounds and white print. It was surprising how unpleasant it was to watch that slide presentation. That firm wasn't selected.

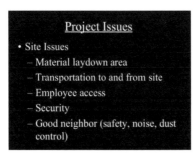

Now, Lori won't say that using those black and white presentation slides was the only reason that firm lost that project (the other firm that was selected did a good presentation), but the unpleasant PowerPoint was one of the first items commented on during the panel discussion process. That poorly designed presentation overwhelmed any good message that the firm tried to communicate.

There are two morals to these stories:

1) your slide may look OK on your computer monitor, but check to see how your slide works through the projector and on the screen.

2) dark slides should be avoided!

Interacting with Visual Aids

1. Control the audience's gaze
Since people read left to right, when possible, presenters should stand to the audience's left of the presentation screen. This way, the gaze comes back to the presenter when the audience is finished with the slide or board.

2. Maximize the amount of time the audience has visual connection with presenters

Slides and boards are competition for presenters. If something is on the screen you're audience is going to read it. So, if you have 6 points, read what's on the slide, then reconnect with the panel to continue the conversation and then go on to the next point. Another option is to reveal the bullet points individually.

3. **Keep an open stance**
   Avoid spending a majority of your time showing a profile to the audience. You can't make a good a connection with the audience that way. Presenters should have one foot parallel to the screen and the other pointing more toward the interview panel (this will resemble the shape of a capital L). This enables you to easily turn at the waist from the screen to the audience without a lot of distracting movement.

4. **If necessary, set up a more appropriate presentation space.**
   Hopefully you have already had an opportunity to view the interview room prior to the interview day. Occasionally, the room provided is not ideally arranged for your interview presentation and may require some minimal modifications. If you find that the interview setup has the panel quite a distance from the screen, ask if you can rearrange the room to bridge the space between the panel and the presenters. If the fixed screen provided is not in the best location for your presentation, bring a portable screen. If there is

insufficient space for your presentation team and the visual aids, ask if you can rearrange some furniture in the room. However, if you make changes in the room for your interview, *make sure to return the room to its original setup prior to departing.*

Possible Boards or Slides:

1. **Organizational chart**

    This helps the panel see the relationships and hierarchy of the project team. Be sure to show your Project Manager as your main point of contact and that both the design and construction phase teams report to him/her. Also indicate which team members cross over from design to construction to show team continuity and understanding of design issues during the construction phase.

2. **Matrix with team experience**

    In addition to slides detailing individual team member experience, provide a matrix that shows the number of comparable projects the individual team members have worked on together.

3. **Site maps, aerials, etc.**

    Most Project Managers and Superintendents do extremely well if you give them something visual to speak about or mark on. It gets them quickly into their comfort zone which is talking about the job.

4. **Project schedule**

   If you are asked to prepare a preliminary project schedule, provide a board or slide that your presenters can use to discuss schedule issues. Make sure, though, that you include an 11" x 17" copy of the schedule at the end of your presentation handout so panel members can read individual line items on the schedule.

5. **Project issues**

   To demonstrate that you have thoroughly studied the project, provide a slide that lists 15 or more project issues, even if you only have time to discuss 5 or 6 in detail. Although the panel members may not have a chance to read every item, this slide illustrates that your team *knows* this project in depth. The next three slides show one very effective way of using this technique.

   "This first slide lists 19 different project issues that our team has identified. As you can see, we've spent significant time thinking about this and we understand the variety of issues that must be addressed to design a successful project."

Question #4 - Project Issues

Interior Issues	Site Issues
Circulation	Sun/shade
Variety of users	Mountain views
Interior views	Soil complications
Technology requirements	Desert wash
Availability of materials	Traffic patterns
Durability of materials	Pedestrian access
Facility maintenance	Xeroscaping
Lighting	Safety in design
Audio/visual equipment	Good neighbor
Office requirements	Noise/light control

"Unfortunately, time does not allow us to discuss all these issues, so we've identified 6 of the most critical challenges that we would like to address in more detail."

Question #4 - Project Issues

Interior Issues	Site Issues
Circulation	Sun/shade
Variety of users	Mountain views
Interior views	*Soil complications*
Technology requirements	Desert wash
Availability of materials	Traffic patterns
Durability of materials	Pedestrian access
Facility maintenance	Xeroscaping
Lighting	*Safety in design*
Audio/visual equipment	Good neighbor
Office requirements	*Noise/light control*

80

"Let's talk about the first one…..Variety of Users".

Question #4 - **Variety of Users**

This facility will require special design for
children, teen, adult and elderly patrons.

• Non-slip, easily maintained flooring
• Specialized furniture (adult and child sized)
• Noise control (kids play area vs. adult reading)
• Specialized lighting
• Computer requirements
• Supervisory requirements

This prior series of slides clearly shows the selection panel
that you are knowledgeable about the project and prepared
to address important project issues.

6. **Why should your team be selected?**
   *This is one of the most critical messages your team must
   convey.* If you can't clearly articulate what makes you
   the best choice, it is going to be difficult for the panel
   to select your team. Use a board or slide to summarize
   the reasons why they should choose you and leave it
   up during the Q & A to reinforce the message.

Let's discuss other visual aids sometimes used in the
presentation:

Samples

- Do not give out things for the selection panel to look at (logs, pictures, material samples) during the presentation. It is distracting for panel members to pass them down the table. This also puts the panelists in the position of having to choose whether to listen to you or look at the items you are handing out.

Handouts

Handouts are a critical tool in the interview process. To use them effectively:

- Prepare handouts for panel members that duplicate your presentation slides. This allows the panel to do less writing and more listening.

- Have light backgrounds on the handout slides so panel members can write notes on the slide.

- Have two presentation slides per page. Do not use the "three per page with note lines" because the slides are so small they are unreadable and frequently unusable for reference.

- Have a separate full-page copy of difficult-to-read items in the back of the handout (i.e. sample project schedules, sample documents, etc.).

- Have enough copies for all expected presenters, panelists, and observers. If allowable, call the owner's interview coordinator and ask how many people will be attending the interview to make sure that enough copies are prepared, and then bring five extra copies just to be on the safe side!

One issue that is often debated is whether to give the handouts to the panel members at the beginning or at the end of the interview presentation. Some believe that handouts should be given at the end so that the panel members don't get distracted looking at the presentation handout instead of the presenter. They also want to avoid having panel members look ahead at the upcoming presentation slides.

Although there is certainly some merit in those concerns, others believe that presentation handouts should be given at the beginning. And here's why…..

- Some panelists have difficulty seeing distances and might not be able to read the boards or screen in the front of the room. Having a handout in front of them makes it easy for them to flip through the presentation with you as you discuss the items on the presentation screen.

- If the handout is provided early, panelists can more easily follow along with the presentation and write questions or notes on the slide page. This can also be a useful reference during the Q & A period and during final deliberations.

- Without a handout, the panelists must write down

everything they want to remember from the presentation. And if panelists are writing down the last thing that you said, there is a good chance that they may miss the next thing that you say!

- If for whatever reason the projector goes out mid-presentation, you can refer the panel directly to the handouts they already have which minimizes the unfortunate disruption.

- If the panelists' minds are going to wander, you are better off letting them look at information in your handout that you want them to see anyway, rather than having them daydream about what they are going to do for dinner that night or when they will be able to go on their next vacation.

- If, on a private sector project, your firm is worried about putting a price for services in the handout for the panelists' premature review, give that one item out as a separate handout when you are ready to discuss price.

- Finally, if panelists receive the handout at the end, it is very likely that they will put it aside without reading it as they get ready for the next interview. Then it is available only as a reference during the discussion period.

It is possible that some panel members will not look at the handout. But for those that do, it is an important convenience that helps them to keep up with your interview. And, by making your presentation more effective, you will make it easier for panelists to give you the most points possible.

So you have crafted compelling content and effective visual aids. You still need the team to deliver the message as intended and in a way that leaves a powerful and positive impression on the panel. That will only happen as a result of effective rehearsals which will be discussed in the next chapter.

NOTES

KEY IDEAS IN THIS CHAPTER:

_____

_____

_____

_____

_____

_____

ACTION ITEMS:

_____

_____

_____

_____

_____

_____

CHAPTER 9

REHEARSING

The best way to ensure you hit your Selection Success target is through disciplined repetition and practice.

When folks are unskilled, uncomfortable or unprepared, they are more likely to make mistakes in the presentation that can send a negative impression to the selection panel. That impression could make the difference between not being selected and selection success.

If you look unprepared, the panel will get the impression that their project doesn't matter to your company. Therefore it is imperative that everyone within your organization be fully committed to doing whatever it takes to get selected.

There are some folks who adamantly refuse to rehearse. Here are some of the excuses that Hilari has heard over the years:

Presenter Excuse 1: "We are builders. Our work should speak for itself."

They already read about you and now they want to hear from you. They are not sold on you. Don't insult the panel by having a "We are too good for this interview" attitude. You won't get selected for sure.

Presenter Excuse 2: "They know us."

Great! And it is likely they know your competition too. Show them you are who they want to work with.

Presenter Excuse 3: "I am an engineer not a speaker."

Absolutely - that's why rehearsing is crucial. It doesn't have to be perfect but preparation maximizes the likelihood that presenters will be effective when they have their one shot to impress the panel. Have you ever seen a film that was not edited? That's because it takes a while to get each scene right. The same is true for presentations.

Presenter Excuse 4: "I'm better just shooting from the hip."

Let me see what you can do just shooting from the hip.

Presenter Excuse 5: "If I rehearse it comes off phony."

Then you are not rehearsing effectively. It should be a conversational, natural, and organized discussion, not a scripted performance.

Presenter Excuse 6: "I'm a game day Quarterback."
I've heard that before from a lot of lazy and unsuccessful presenters.

Presenter Excuse 7: "I can't leave the job site."
You won't have a job to go to if you don't get more work. Find someone to cover.

Presenter Excuse 8: "I don't have time to rehearse."
See answer above.

Presenter Excuse 9: "The words are on the PowerPoint so I'm set."
See previous chapter.

For many presenters, the level of enthusiasm for interview rehearsals is rivaled only by that of going to the dentist. But rehearsals are absolutely necessary!

Practice builds confidence, consistency, clarity and conviction. Interview rehearsal leads to successful presenting on Interview Day.

Like going to the gym, one good workout isn't going to make you fit. It requires discipline and repetition to build your presentation muscle. But form is also important. Practice the right way and you will see results. Give 100% in rehearsal so you can repeat it during the interview. That is how professional athletes are able to perform come game day. They practice for success. Interview teams must as well.

Rehearse your presentation more than you think you need to. Get so comfortable with the words that the presentation becomes natural and you don't have to consciously think about what you are supposed to say next.

We're not suggesting that you memorize every word that will come out of your mouth. The delivery should appear spontaneous and genuine. However, we recommend committing to memory: your outline of key points, your opening, closing, power statements and "What's In It For Them" (discussed in Chapter 7). You'll get more bang for your presentation buck.

Remember, practice builds confidence, consistency, clarity and conviction.

It's important that each presenter know exactly what he or she will discuss in the interview, but it is also critical to have the presentation team actually practice the presentation together. This can help in the following ways:

- Outlining your part and knowing what you want to say is very different than speaking it out loud. Verbalizing your thoughts will help crystallize your presentation.

- By hearing other members give their presentation, it will

make it easier for team members to listen for any gaps or overlaps in information presented.

- Team members can ensure that they have smooth transitions between speakers and between questions.

- The team members should practice when they will stand and sit, and how they will move during the presentation.

We suggest that you create a mock panel. Have experienced outside consultants or even other firm members act as panelists during the interview practice to provide critical feedback to the presentation team. Are they answering all parts of every question? Do the presenters speak clearly (too fast, too slow, too quietly)? Do the presenters connect with the interview panel (eye contact, show some personality)?

Using your firm's employees on a mock panel is not only useful in providing valuable feedback to the team preparing for the interview, but it is also good experience for company employees who may be on a future interview presentation team. This will allow the mock panelists to gain some insight on how presentations are viewed from the selection panel side of the table.

Use a stop watch to time every rehearsal. The goal is to build consistency and clarity in the allotted time without rushing the presentation. If presenters speak very quickly in an attempt to cram extra content, they will usually end up shooting themselves in the foot. When going on vacation, you can't fit your entire closet in a single suitcase. You have to make choices that will fit the space available. The same is true for presentations. You will have significantly more speaking material that the time will allow. By rushing, the words start to blend together and it is likely the audience will not retain information spoken in rapid fire. *Don't rush your words, make content more concise.*

Create ground rules for the rehearsals:

- Interview rehearsal is non-negotiable. Each presenter must attend. Get coverage on job sites.

- While sometimes you need to attend to other business responsibilities, it is a good idea to limit cell phone use during presentation preparation sessions. Plan scheduled breaks so participants can respond to voice mail, etc.. A lot of time is wasted with people taking calls, coming in and out of rehearsal sessions.

Here are some proven strategies to make the most out of available rehearsal time:

<u>Start with a Talk-Through Session</u>

- Talk through each individual presentation segment.

- Identify the overall time allotted for each question and how long each person will have to speak.

- Have the team offer suggestions to refine the content and create visual components to enhance the message.

- Then do a second talk through to better identify each member's presentation part.

Individual/Partner Rehearsal

- Practice for real! Stand and deliver it.

- Each person should find a space to run through their sequence alone three times. Then have the team divide into groups of two and have each member present to their partner.

- Each person should do their sequence three times for their partner. Partners will keep time and offer feedback. This way you will know if you may need to cut or add content.

Group Rehearsal I

- Reconvene the group.

- Stage your rehearsals to resemble the actual presentation space.

- Decide if each speaker will move their own slides or if you will have someone else do it.

- Do two complete run-throughs. If you are using boards, practice with them. The more comfortable your speakers are with all elements of the presentation, the better off they will be.

- Each speaker's segment should be timed so that the speakers know if they need to add or modify their content.

- After each speaker, offer feedback and suggestions to fine-tune content.

- Work on delivery to make sure the message and messengers are compelling.

In Between Group Practice Sessions

- Before the next rehearsal, each presenter should practice their part in smaller chunks to get more comfortable. It's more effective to practice one slide at a time or by repeating two minutes of a presentation and getting it down, before moving on to work on the next two minutes of the presentation.

- *Repetition is critical to presentation success!* Participants should practice their sequence out loud several times before the group practices again. You can do it driving to work. Another option is to find a friend or colleague and do three run-throughs back-to back (If your sequence is five minutes, this will take you no more than twenty minutes per session).

Group Rehearsal II

- Stage your rehearsals to resemble the actual presentation space.

- Practice for real! Use available visual elements.

- Do a minimum of two complete run-throughs, using available visual aids and transitions between speakers.

- Each speaker's segment should be timed so that the speakers know if they still need to add or modify their content.

- After each speaker, offer feedback and suggestions to fine-tune content.

- Work on delivery to make sure the message and messengers are compelling.

- Invite a mock panel to view the presentation and offer constructive feedback and pose challenging questions to the participants.

- Spend time identifying anticipated questions and practicing responses to potential questions.

- If you have kept track of questions asked in previous interviews with this owner, use these to help the team practice their responses.

When possible, avoid making major last-minute changes. Occasionally it is necessary to redirect segments of the interview. But sometimes changes can make a stressful situation more challenging. Keep in mind that less skilled presenters can require more time to adjust to changes.

Rehearsing is required for interview day success. That

success depends on the message but also how effectively your messengers deliver the message in relation to the other competitors.

NOTES

KEY IDEAS IN THIS CHAPTER:

_____

_____

_____

_____

_____

_____

ACTION ITEMS:

_____

_____

_____

_____

_____

_____

CHAPTER 10

DELIVERY

B oth the message and the messenger influence the impression left on the panel. Yet all too often, presentation teams forget that the selection committee will be getting a whole lot of information over the course of several hours from many qualified candidates. Your team and your message need to be memorable and effective.

Delivery is the execution of the presentation message. It is the personality of your presentation.

Delivery is what made the difference between the teacher that put you to sleep and the one that kept you engaged and excited about learning.

In Chapter 6, we shared the quote by Maya Angelou, "People will forget what you said, people will forget what you did, but people will never forget how you made them feel."

At the end of interview day, after they have had several hours of presentations, the selection panel will likely not remember EVERYTHING your team said or did. They WILL remember how you made them feel. And by being more engaging, your selection panel, your clients and your peers will remember MORE of what you said, more of what you did, and they will remember YOU more favorably — increasing the likelihood of selection success.

Does delivery matter? Absolutely…..especially if you want to be remembered in a positive way.

A good analogy is food. The message is the actual food while delivery is the experience – plate presentation, atmosphere, ambiance, and service.

For example, a fast food burger is thrown together in a paper box and handed to us from a drive-through window with fries and ketchup that comes oozing out of a package. The basic ingredients are the same as the burger you might have at a sit-down restaurant that offers cloth napkins with smiling, attentive servers who bring your burger served open face on a plate with fries, a slice of orange to garnish the plate. Each is a different experience that is shaped by the context in which the meal takes place. Similarly, delivery influences the message by impacting what the panel members see, hear, and feel.

In addition to shading the message and enhancing retention, your delivery reveals many important characteristics of your team to the selection committee:

• What the people behind the presentation are like

• What this team brings and what qualities the individual team members possess

• If the team is passionate about the project

• If the team is easy to get along with

• If the team seems like a cohesive unit

• If the team truly understands project issues and owner concerns

• If your team is a good fit for them on this project

The following tips will immediately elevate the effectiveness of your delivery.

1. Who should speak?

• If the Principal of the firm would like to be part of the interview presentation, depending on how much time the firm has for their presentation, give the Principal only two to five minutes at the beginning to offer welcoming remarks and assurances that all required resources will be available to make sure that this project is a success. Then the Principal should introduce the Project Manager and hand the presentation off to him/her.

- Your Project Manager should make a majority of the presentation. The panel wants to hear from the person who will be their "day-to-day person" throughout the project, not the business development person or the head of the firm.

- It's important that you bring your key people to the interview so that the panel gets a chance to see and hear from them personally. If you have a question about who to bring to the interview, take a good look at the interview questions. For design consultants, in addition to the Project Manager and the Design Engineer/Architect, if there's a question regarding the budget and cost control, bring your Cost Estimator. If there's a question regarding specific project challenges, bring the people best qualified to address those issues (mechanical engineer, geotechnical engineer, audiovisual consultant, security consultant, etc.). For a CM@Risk, the Project Manager, Superintendent and Cost Estimator are critical presenters.

- What do you do if a critical team member (project manager, project architect, design engineer, superintendent, key subconsultant, etc.) is not available at the interview time? It depends on the situation and on the size of the project you are interviewing for :

  - For a standard size project:

    - If your critical person is committed to a meeting on their current project and cannot get away for the interview, the Principal/Project Manager should explain to the selection panel that the person has a commitment to their current client that they cannot break. But let the panel know that although it is certainly unfortunate for this interview, this is the kind of dedication you have for your clients…..the same kind of dedication you will show to this new client if your firm is selected for this project. Then have a qualified substitute handle their part of the interview.

❑ If your critical person is on vacation but still in town, really try to get them to the interview. But if they can't make it (out-of-town, ill, or otherwise committed), let the panel know that they would like to be there but that they are unavailable. One possible idea is to videotape them giving at least part of their presentation and play that during the interview. This lets the panel get a feel for that person and shows them that you made the extra effort to involve them in the interview process.

◆ For a really large project:

❑ It is somewhat less critical to have the design manager or the superintendent at the presentation, but it is *really* important that your project manager attend the interview. You are surely up against other very qualified firms and your missing project manager will put you at a significant disadvantage that can be almost impossible to overcome. If you really want the project, do everything you can to have the PM there, even if you have to fly him back from his vacation spot for the presentation day. If it's just impossible to get the PM there, try doing the video presentation and/or have him on a conference call speaker phone at the interview.

◆ Have the key team members at the interview. Bringing a bunch of people does not automatically show commitment to the project....it could give the impression that this will be an expensive team. Look at the questions in the interview letter and consider what your team has identified as critical issues, then bring the team members who can best address those items. Unless there is a specific question or challenge regarding survey issues or soil testing, don't bring the more general subconsultants to the presentation. Ideally, everyone who comes should have a part in the presentation.

◆ Have key personnel address questions regarding their sections of the interview (i.e. the Project Designer should address design challenges; the Scheduling Supervisor should discuss the proposed project schedule; the Cost Estimator should address project budget issues; the Superintendent should address site challenges).

2. Eye contact

Eye contact is a critical tool for building a connection with your selection panel. Avoid trying to cover everyone in one fell swoop – otherwise known as the sprinkler effect. Hold eye contact 3-4 seconds per person. Hold the gaze! Hold the gaze! Hold the gaze!   This does three things:

• It creates more of a feeling of having a series of small conversations rather than giving a presentation.

• It has a calming effect (similar to that of holding your gaze on a single spot if you are experiencing motion sickness). It reduces nerves by keeping the presenter's focus on the audience and reduces the presenter's self-consciousness.

• Eye contact increases presenter likeability and trustworthiness.

Try to hold your eye contact for one to two sentences. Rehearse in your practice sessions. Make it a series of individual conversations as opposed to trying to cover everyone at once.

3. Look interested

Don't just say you want the job. Let us see it in your face and hear it in your voice. Do you appear as if you are interested in the project and do you appear as if you care? Is there a twinkle of excitement in the eyes of the team members that indicates they really want the job?

4. Smile

Is it appropriate to smile? Absolutely...as long as it is not a permanent toothy grin resembling The Joker from Batman. A sincere, natural smile not only puts others at ease it also puts the presenter at ease. In an interview, what does a smile say? What message does it deliver to your panel? It says that you're relaxed, comfortable and glad to be interviewing. It says that you enjoy what you do. It might also suggest that you enjoy the people that you work with and that you bring a little bit something extra to this particular project – passion for your work. Passionate people go above and beyond the call of duty.

5. Posture

Avoid slouching in the chair or leaning back in your seat like you are at home watching a football game. Be conscious of your posture from the moment you enter the presentation space until you walk out the door. Ideally, you should have their stomach in, chest up, shoulders back, and head up.

6. Don't rush your first words

As you make your way to the front of the presentation space, plant your feet, make solid eye contact with a couple of people on the panel, take a relaxed breath in and out, THEN speak. This will take no more than a couple of seconds.

7. Make it a conversation

You do not want to come across as though you were preaching to or instructing the panel.   Work to make your interview conversational rather than a stiff and formal presentation. Make it *feel* more like a dialogue than a monologue.

8. Diction

You've worked too hard on the presentation to walk in and have the selection committee be unable to understand what you're saying because team members sound like they have marbles in their mouths. Therefore it is imperative that presenters practice good diction in and out of presentation settings – on the phone, at home, and on the job site..…PLUS speaking with good diction makes us sound smarter.

9. Vary vocal inflection, pace, and pauses

Help your selection panel retain more information by having some vocal variation in your presentation. Lack of inflection makes it really hard for your audience to follow along and easy for them to drift off. By varying tones, your voice acts as a tour guide that directs the audience to what is important. Slowing down the pace and rhythm or adding a pause adds emphasis to what is articulated. A deliberate pause can be quite powerful in the appropriate moment. By infusing some vocal variation, adding some pauses, and slowing yourself down, you're helping your selection panel remember more of what you have to say.

10. Volume

It is important to adjust your volume to the room. One of the reasons to visit the presentation space in advance of interview day is to test acoustics and sound. If there is an echo, you may need to lower volume. If there is a noisy air conditioning unit, you may need to raise the volume.

11. Listen well

How well you listen in the interview reveals to the selection panel how you might listen if you were awarded the job. Demonstrate good listening when other presenters are speaking as well as in the Q & A sequence. The panel is not just paying attention to the person who's speaking but will also notice the other team members. It is amazing how many stories that we've heard about team members that were checking text messages, jotting notes, or picking their fingernails while a member of their team was presenting. What does that say about someone's attitude toward this project, toward their teammates, or toward the panel? Nothing good.

12. Presence

One element that's an intangible is something that we call "presence." By presence we're not referring to stage presence, which some presenters have. The presence we're referring to is actually being in the moment -- being fully present and engaged with the panel. There are presenters who appear almost to be standing and reading words off the back of the room, fearful that eye contact with the panel will cause them to forget who they are and what they know. They're not actually present. Or they're thinking two sentences ahead or two paragraphs ahead.

You can't make a connection with the selection committee if your focus is on future.   You can't connect if you're thinking about the past, *"Oh my gosh, I just messed that up."* Rehearse enough so that you can be present and confident in what you are saying.

13. Show that you genuinely care about the project
Is this just another job or does that panel sense you really *want* to be their partner on this project.

14. Unpretentiousness
Avoid chest beating and arrogance. Even if you KNOW you are best for the job, there is a way to be confident without being cocky. Occasionally, nervousness comes off as stiffness and inapproachability. Hilari was invited to assist a local construction firm after they received disconcerting feedback regarding their Project Manager during a debriefing session. The panelist had indicated that the major reason they weren't selected was because the Project Manager came across as arrogant, cold, very difficult to work with, and just seemed to have a chip on his shoulder. What's interesting is that this is the nicest fellow you could ever meet. When you sit down across the table from him he's obviously pleasant and loves what he does. Get him talking about one of his projects and he is genuine and totally unpretentious. Yet on that particular interview, he wasn't well rehearsed. He became extremely nervous, and his nervousness was interpreted as coldness, stiffness, and arrogance by the panel. This was not somebody the selection panel thought they could work well with so the firm was not selected.

15. Like and trust

Do you buy from folks that you don't like or trust? Absolutely not! So why would the selection panel hire you if what you are projecting is not likeable or trustworthy. As we mentioned earlier, they will not forget how you made them feel. Look the panel members in the eye, show that you know the project, and let them see your desire to be selected.

16. Be confident about what you know

Hilari had an opportunity to work with a firm competing for a major project. The Superintendent, who was not the most polished presenter, was the member of the team who really made the difference because he came across incredibly knowledgeable, likable, and displayed so much passion for the project when he spoke. This is a reminder that you are not expected to be a professional speaker, but you must bring knowledge and enthusiasm to the interview. It doesn't have to be polished, it doesn't have to be perfect, but it should be personable.

Now, here are some common pitfalls to avoid:

- **Over-using the words "guys" or "men"**

Hilari was preparing a team that had an interview for a large data center. The project manager was describing the challenge of having a number of workers in a small area. He said, "We will have 120 men in the building. One way to avoid a heavy concentration is by having a swing shift."

Hilari asked if all of the people working would be male. He said that, while there would mostly be men on the job, some women would also be working. It would be more appropriate to refer to them as workers or electricians."

- **"I'm going to tell you about"**
This can be an over-used and often unnecessary transition.

For example: "My name is Mike and I will be your Project Superintendent. Today I am going to tell you about my experience. I have been in the construction industry for 20 years." Deleting those unnecessary words strengthens what is being said. "My name is Mike and I will be your Project Superintendent. I have been in the construction industry for 20 years."

The only person who should use words like these should be the person who is doing the presentation preview, the Principal or Project Manager. "In response to questions you provided, over the next 30 minutes you will get to know our team, we will address our experience on comparable projects, discuss our approach to pre-construction services, project understanding and approach, and demonstrate why we are the best fit to ensure a successful project."

- **Reading the Panel**
Most folks misinterpret what they see if they are excited or nervous. Let's say someone on the selection panel is

looking down and writing. They don't look at you while you are speaking and seem to not be paying attention. If you focus too hard on getting them to pay attention, you end up alienating the rest of the panel. Why not assume that person is so interested in the great things that you are saying they want to keep good notes? That's a much more powerful place for you to be in as opposed to worrying "Do they like me, do they like me, oh my gosh, she's not watching me so I bet she doesn't like me." and letting it kill your presentation. Assume they like you.

Now that your team's delivery is sharp, you are ready for interview day.

NOTES

KEY IDEAS IN THIS CHAPTER:

_____

_____

_____

_____

_____

_____

ACTION ITEMS:

_____

_____

_____

_____

_____

_____

CHAPTER 11

INTERVIEW DAY

The big day is here. You have been rehearsing and the team is ready. *Unless absolutely necessary, do not make any changes to the presentation the day of the interview.* Last minute changes can throw off unseasoned presenters.

Ensure your team is solid on interview day with the following tips:

1. Interview-day rehearsing

Don't over-do it. It should be fresh and energetic. Over-rehearsing on the day of the interview can diminish energy and enthusiasm. You don't want the team appearing like they are on auto-pilot. Depending on your scheduled interview time, do one or two run-throughs so that your team members are comfortable with their part of the interview.

On interview day, we recommend spending some additional time rehearsing questions and answers. Although the team has worked on this during rehearsals, you can never be too prepared for Q & A.

2. Make sure you have everything you need

Here is a check-list:

- Boards

- Easels

- Lap-tops (bring two in case you run into a problem. Make sure they are both fully charged.)

- Someone who *knows* how to hook up the computer and projector quickly.

- Zip drive with the presentation

- Projectors (even if they provide one, it is best to use your own. Theirs should be back-up)

- Portable projector screen

- Handouts

3. Have an emergency kit with essentials

- Spray wrinkle remover (in case someone gets wrinkled on the drive)

- Duct tape (tape computer and projector cords to the ground to avoid tripping and acrobatics)

- Water (room temperature is best)

- Comb
- Brush
- Hair spray
- Instant Shoe Shine (you can get this at any shoe store or drug store, Target, Wal-Mart)

4. Dress appropriately

- Make sure the team is pleasant to look at and they dress in a way that appears respectful of the panel.
- Dress appropriate to your position
  - ◆ executives and managers should consider a coat and tie;
  - ◆ designers and superintendents should consider Dockers and either button-down shirt or golf shirt with company logo.
- Don't look like you just walked off the job site.
- Try to have the team members dress in the same color family (ex. grays, blues, browns)
- Clothing should be neatly pressed.
- Shoes should look clean.

5. Food and beverages

- Avoid excessive caffeine. It can exacerbate nervous energy. Presenters don't want to appear edgy, too hyper or aggressive.
- Avoid carbonated beverages two hours before the

presentation. There is nothing more embarrassing or uncomfortable than burping in the middle of a presentation.

- Avoid dairy products the day of the interview. They cause an increase in mucous production.

- Avoid spicy food or anything that can cause you indigestion, especially if you have a nervous stomach.

- Avoid onions and garlic.

- Drink plenty of room temperature water to avoid dry mouth.

- If you need cough drops or hard candy before the interview, make sure they are clear and don't leave a colored stain on the tongue. Don't use them during the presentation!

- Don't over-do the fluids before the interview. It isn't easy to take a potty break mid-presentation and you don't want to be uncomfortable while interviewing.

6. Getting to the interview

- Allow plenty of driving time. Drive together if possible (including subconsultants). This helps build energy, chemistry and keeps folks from talking on cell phones before the interview.

- On the drive to the interview laugh, listen to music, make it fun. If you feel good, relaxed, and present, you are better able to be personable and in the moment.

Like in sports, being rigid and non-present can have unfortunate results. Effective presenters have rehearsed enough that they can let go and make the presentation a conversation.

- Leave cell phones in the car.

7. **Arrive 30 minutes before the interview to allow for:**

- Restroom runs.
- Relaxation.
- A team pep talk.
- Time for each individual to get centered, focused and comfortable.

8. **First impressions**

- *You are "on" as soon as you step out of the car.* You never know when a member of the panel may be watching.

- *Your attitude sets the tone for the interview.* Rather than taking the approach that an interview is a treacherous thing, walk in as if the members of the selection panel are people who you already know, trust and like – and that they know, trust, and like you! This increased confidence will show in your manner and be heard in your voice throughout the presentation.

- *Smile and make eye contact as you enter the room.* Look like you are enthusiastic, sincerely excited about the project and proud of the company you represent.

A genuine smile makes us feel good and puts others at ease.

- *Body language and movement tell a story.* The selection panel will begin forming an impression about your team before a word is uttered. Be aware of the messages your body language may be sending.

9. Setting up and taking down boards or PowerPoint

During the interview rehearsals, come up with your set up strategy and practice it. Assign who will be responsible for doing what. Have easels extended before you enter the presentation room to make set-up more efficient. Once invited into the interview room, set up quickly. Distribute presentation handouts to the panel members and observers.

10. Keeping time

Staying within your allotted time shows not only that you can follow directions, but it also shows respect for the panel and their process.

- During the final two rehearsals, you should have kept a time log per slide. Use the log to get a sense of whether you are on track, going too fast or going over time.

- Identify one person to be responsible for keeping time in the presentation. Devise a system to alert presenters that they are exceeding their allotted time. Use a signal (hand on face, minimally tapping watch, time cards) to let presenters know that they are going too long. One creative and effective option is to have your timekeeper carefully flash a laser pointer on the wall above and behind the selection panel. The panel won't see it, but your team member will absolutely get the message.

- The timing device should be silent, preferably a stop watch or something that counts seconds. Lori remembers an interview where the timekeeper placed an egg timer on the table and set the timer for each speaker. Unfortunately, as Lori confirmed with a number of the selection panel members, it was difficult to stay focused on the presentation because that egg timer kept tick, tick, tick, tick, ticking on the table in front of them!

- If a panel member interrupts your presentation with a question, try to answer the question thoroughly but as quickly as possible in order to get back on track and complete the presentation on time.

11. Don't sit too close to panel members
Give the panel members some room to write without worrying about interview team members viewing their comments or ratings.

12. Introduce everyone that you bring
That means everyone……including the computer operator or the business development person who may be acting as the interview timer.

13. Organization chart and name tags

Have an organization chart out or easily available for the selection panel to reference during the presentation, and use name tags. Also, make sure that the first time someone speaks during the presentation that they re-introduce themselves so the panel doesn't have to search for the presenter's name in the handout or in their notes.

14. Stand during your presentation

Presenters should stand during their part of a formal presentation. Unless invited to do so by the owner, the concept of "let's just sit down across the table from each other and chat" generally does not go over very well (it's too informal and difficult to use presentation tools effectively).

15. Non-speaking team members

When they are not presenting, the other team members should focus their attention on the individual speaking. Focusing on the presenter shows respect for their team member and will encourage the panel to direct their attention to the speaker as well. Avoid flipping through notes, whispering to other team members. Also, avoid focusing on individual panel members during the presentation portion of the interview as this could make them uncomfortable.

16. Have fun and enjoy the opportunity.

Coming into the interview with a pleasant demeanor and positive attitude helps to build rapport with the selection panel. This will make it a more pleasant experience for both the presenters and the panelists and will increase your chance of Selection Success!

By following these suggestions, you are well on your way to an incredible interview. After you nail that, you must nail the Q & A!

NOTES

KEY IDEAS IN THIS CHAPTER:

_____

_____

_____

_____

_____

_____

ACTION ITEMS:

_____

_____

_____

_____

_____

_____

CHAPTER 12

MASTERFULLY MANAGING Q & A

Your team has made it to the home stretch. But the last leg of the race requires precision and focus. Crashing and burning in the Question & Answer period is like being in the lead going into the last leg of a track and field relay only to drop the baton.

A great presentation can be nullified by poor Q & A. It is vital to interview success and is the primary opportunity to engage in an interactive dialogue with the selection committee.

This is, however, the part of your interview that is unknown. The panel could ask anything. It is for this reason that rehearsing potential questions is imperative. The goal of Q & A rehearsal is to challenge the team with a range of possible questions so they will be adequately prepared and comfortable answering questions about almost anything. Ask the toughest questions as well as the most mundane.

Ask questions that make sense and ones that don't. Ask questions that challenge them with worst case scenarios and others they can answer easily.

The manner in which you respond demonstrates how the team will handle client concerns when they arise. Will you be evasive, combative, or defensive? Or will you exhibit caring, resolve, and poise?

In an interview process, there can be three kinds of questions to expect:

- Interview letter questions – these are generally questions that take time to prepare and may have multiple parts. The interview presentation should be created around these and must address every part of every question included in the interview letter.

- Standard questions asked during the Q & A period – these are questions that will be asked to each of the firms being interviewed. These questions let the panel know what your team members *really* know about the project without having days or weeks to craft an answer.

- Firm-specific questions asked during the Q & A period – these are specific questions that the panel will ask to an individual firm usually to follow up on something that they either saw in the firm's Statement of Qualifications, they've heard in the interview, or they found in checking references.

Here are 22 ways to help you increase the likelihood of Q & A success:

1. Rehearse, rehearse, rehearse. This will help your presenters maintain the concentration, balance, and agility critical to Q & A success.

2. Maintain poise, posture, and good eye contact.

3. Keep a record of questions from previous interviews and sort them by client. Use these to rehearse in mock Q & A sessions because owners will often reuse Q & A questions.

4. Designate a scribe to record the questions being asked during the actual interview. Not only will this will be useful in future Q & A practices, but it will give you additional insight into the owner's concerns when you are selected for the project.

5. Unless a selection panel member specifically directs a question to one specific interview team member, have the Project Manager field the questions and hand them off to the most appropriate person. The PM can also "tee up" the answer to point his team in the right direction, "Joe and I were talking about that when we walked the site last week. Joe, why don't you tell them about the two drainage ideas we came up with."

6. Don't have one person on the interview team (whether it is the Principal or the Project Manager) try to answer every question asked. It shows poor teamwork and it is unlikely that one person will know the best answer to every question.

7. The panel usually has limited time for the question and answer period so listen closely to the question being asked by the panel member and keep your answers short and to the point. Answer the question as simply as possible.

8. Look interested in answering their question and confident in your ability to respond. Keep a positive attitude and know you have the capacity to answer any question they may throw at you.

9. Resist formulating your response until you have heard the entire question. Patiently listen and earmark primary issues or key ideas to address in your response. If you formulate the response in your head before you have heard the question fully, you will likely provide an inaccurate response or one that comes across canned or unnatural.

10. Start and end your response with your eyes connecting to the individual who asked the question. Use the panelist's name. Direct most of the response to the person who asked the question.

11. If you don't understand the question being asked it is perfectly acceptable to:

- Ask the panelist to repeat the question.

- Ask for clarification (i.e., Are you looking for a better understanding of how we establish contingency fees?) Occasionally, a question may be worded poorly or confusing. You might respond by saying, "Help me understand, are you really looking for information about ___ or about ___?" If you give them two options, sometimes it helps to direct their mind to what really matters.

- Rephrase the question asked prior to responding.

- At the end of your response, ask, "Did that answer your question?" But do not do this each time you respond. Save it in your back pocket in case you are uncertain if you completely answered the question to their satisfaction.

12. If you feel like you are not clear about how to respond, do not answer immediately. Pause. It is better to become clear by asking them to repeat the question rather than risking an incorrect response.

13. Slow down your rate of speaking slightly to help maintain composure and clarity of thought.

14. Have no more than one person add to the response.

This is critical since piling on makes the person that initially answered the question appear less competent.

15. Answer truthfully. However, when possible, use a positive angle in the response.

    For example: "We have not worked with our partner, ML Construction before. However, we have had tremendous respect for each other for many years and have been looking for the right project. This is the perfect project for us to partner on. Together we bring you, the City of Phoenix, a tremendous team that has the collective experience and enthusiasm that will ensure a successful project. We have no doubt that we will work well together and that you will be the first of many clients pleased with our partnership."

16. Make sure team members who aren't responding to the question asked remain respectful and engaged. Team members need to stay positive, poised and attentive to whoever is speaking.

17. Use real examples to demonstrate a process. By telling a real story, you will help make your message more concrete: "On the State Street project, we demonstrated our ability to serve our clients through creative value engineering. For example…"

18. If it is a complex or multiple part question, it is okay to:

- Request that the person asking the question break it up for you so you can answer each part individually.

- Answer the part you are most comfortable with first then go on to another part of the question. It is okay to answer the second part first then go back to the first part. Just let them know you are doing that.

- Pause before answering. It is better to collect your thoughts at the beginning rather than rambling aimlessly before getting to the point.

19. If you can't answer the question with the information you currently have available, don't make something up. Instead, try relating it to a similar project you've completed, such as "That is a great question. Based on the information available, any response we might provide would be speculative. However, based on our experience with some comparable projects...."

20. Although it is unlikely that a selection panelist will ask a detailed question regarding a relatively obscure issue, if they do and that subconsultant is not present, see if one of the attending team members can respond intelligently to the question. If not, let the panel know that you don't have that information immediately available, but rather than give incorrect information, the firm will follow up on that question immediately upon

leaving the interview and have a written answer to them by ___ time (one hour, right after lunch, by the end of the interview day, etc.). It is better to admit that you do not have that information at this moment and get the correct information to the panel as soon as possible, than to try to "wing it" and give an incorrect answer.

21. Differentiate yourself from your competitors, but avoid saying anything negative about your competition or former clients.

22. Don't get defensive even if the interviewer is rough on you. Do your best to stay as respectful as possible.

Now that you have concluded the interview with an effective Q & A session, you must patiently wait for the panel to deliberate and make their selection. You might use this time to have an in-house discussion on your interview performance and to think about a debriefing session with the client.

<u>NOTES</u>

KEY IDEAS IN THIS CHAPTER:

_____

_____

_____

_____

_____

_____

ACTION ITEMS:

_____

_____

_____

_____

_____

_____

CHAPTER 13

DEBRIEF TIPS

I t can be extremely frustrating for your presentation team to put forth so much time and effort and not get selected.

How many times have you heard: "It was so close! You were second!" After losing a project interview, those words are about as comforting as, "You *almost* won an Olympic Gold Medal."

Most of us have heard the proverb, "If at first you don't succeed, try, try again." But, as Albert Einstein noted, *"Insanity is doing the same thing over and over again and expecting different results."*

Therefore, it makes sense to learn how you can refine your project interview approach and use each experience for leverage.

Golfer Ben Hogan once said, *"The most important shot in golf is the next one."* Your most important project interview is the next one.   So, make the most of it!

One of my clients equated Project Interviewing to his golf game, "There is always room for improvement and sometimes, making a few minor adjustments to your game can make a world of difference."

Win or lose, here are ways to make sure that you benefit from each interview.

1. Record Interview Details
For each client, create a folder for each interview. Include any information that might help you prepare for future interviews with this client: the shortlist letter, a list of interview participants, the rehearsal schedule, panel members and presentation room details.   You may interview in that same space in the future, so it is a good idea to draw a floor plan that includes the location of tables, seats, doors, windows, the projection screen, etc.

This is critical: Write down each question that was asked during Q & A along with your response. The participants should discuss the responses with your Marketing/ Business Development team and your Interview Preparation Consultant.   This process will help you find opportunities to improve future responses to similar questions. You can also use these questions to help future interview teams prepare for interviews with the same client. Since you can lose a job in Q & A, practicing this interview element is critical.

2. Track Progress with an Interview Journal. Note what worked and what needs refinement. For each team member, identify the most prominent strengths and key areas for improvement.

3. More Do's and Don'ts

Do   *Ask for a debrief whether you win or lose.*
If your team was not selected, a post-interview debrief can be an excellent opportunity to learn from the owner where you were on-target and where you may have been off. Consider debriefing an additional opportunity to enhance a relationship, connect and make a favorable impression. Every loss can become an opportunity if you learn from it.

If you won, you don't really need to set up a separate debriefing meeting; just ask if you can have a few minutes after the scope of work meeting for some debriefing comments. There's a good chance that there is something that you did especially well or could have done better.

Don't *Ask for a debrief every single time*, especially if you submit a lot of SOQ's or do multiple interviews with a client in a short period of time.   However, you should ask the owner to discuss your strengths and weaknesses if it was your first time interviewing with that owner or if you thought you were particularly well qualified for the job.

Do *Call the client and make an appointment* for a brief, 15-20 minute meeting. While it may not always be practical, it is best to debrief in person. However, if they seem reluctant to meet, ask when it might be convenient to discuss this over the phone.

Don't *Just drop in and ask "for a couple of minutes".* The owner's selection managers tend to be very busy people. If you just drop in, one of four things will happen:

- ◆ They'll be delighted for the interruption in their busy day (not very likely).

- ◆ They'll say "no" because they are too busy which will be uncomfortable for both of you.

- ◆ They'll say "OK" but do so reluctantly which doesn't help build a positive relationship.

- ◆ They'll say "OK" but rush through the debrief in order to get back to what they were scheduled to do.

Do *Try to schedule a debrief as soon as possible.* It can be difficult for anyone to recollect in detail events from a month ago. If it appears that you may be unable to meet for a while, consider asking a few of the questions you want to discuss and kindly ask your contact to jot a few ideas down for your meeting.

Don't *Wait too long to ask for a debrief.* Be mindful that too much time in between the interview and the debrief discussion may alter the feedback.

Do *Bring a maximum of three people to the debrief.* These could include the Principal, the Project Manager and/or the Marketing Coordinator. They can share debriefing comments to the rest of the team.

Don't *Bring too many people.* It can be uncomfortable for the owner's representative to be facing a lot of people in these meetings and you want to make the owner as comfortable as possible. This way, it is more likely that they will be forthright in their criticisms and willing to make suggestions to help you improve your SOQ and interview presentation.

Do *Encourage the owner to be candid and brutally honest.* This is not the time for them to be gentle or concerned about hurting your feelings. You need them to be as up front with you as possible. Ask what you did well and where you could improve.

Don't *Expect to only get positive comments.* If you're only hearing good things, chances are that the owner's representative is not being completely candid with you. Prompt the owner with questions that specifically ask for areas of improvement.

Do *Come prepared with questions.* Bring a list of open-ended questions to help stimulate conversation. Keep your questions targeted so you can get useful feedback:

- Positive or negative, what three words would best describe the impression our team left on the panel?

- What could we have done differently?

- What did we do right?

- What elements had the greatest impact on your selection?

- Are there any upcoming projects that you think we might be good candidates for?

Don't *Leave it to the owner to carry the discussion.* The more you make this a conversation, the more comfortable and open the owner will likely be.

Do *Assume that the owner knows what they are talking about.* Chances are that the owner's representative has good experience in reviewing SOQs and viewing interviews, and if you can get them to open up, you will likely hear some really useful information.

Don't *Get defensive and don't try to justify your presentation!* It doesn't matter what you meant to say or if you disagree with their comments…..all that matters is how the owners viewed what you provided. If the owner did not understand what you were trying to convey, ask them how you might have addressed this to make it clearer.

4. And finally:

• *Be pleasant, smile!* William Fay, a Public Works Director, said "You can't win a past project at a debrief, but you can lose the next one!" Make sure that you let the owner know that you are not there to complain, but that you value their advice and want to learn how to improve. You don't want the owner to feel that he has to be on the defensive and justify the panel's decision.

• *Remember that these are not easy conversations to have.* Nobody likes being the bearer of bad news. It can be difficult for some owners to explain what the panel thought about your firm's presentation, particularly when they are identifying things that did not go over well. But ironically, it can also be difficult to explain why a firm wasn't selected despite the fact that they did a great interview. Sometimes the truth is that there were a number of good, qualified firms interviewing for

141

this project and that the panel just went with another company.   We know it is hard, but don't press too much.

- *Thank the owner for taking the time to meet with you.* As we said, they are busy people and these are generally not easy meetings to have. Show them that you appreciate their effort and their advice.

- *Let them know that*:

   - you appreciated the opportunity to interview

   - you are very interested in working with that owner

   - you look forward to the chance to interview with them in the future.

- Make the recommended changes! If you don't take advantage of what you have learned, you have wasted both your time and the time the owner took to meet with you.

By taking full advantage of the debriefing process and learning how to improve your Statement of Qualifications submittals and interview presentations, you will have a better view of the target, improve your aim, increase the confidence of your team, and build consistency. All of these will help increase your Selection Success!

NOTES

KEY IDEAS IN THIS CHAPTER:

_____

_____

_____

_____

_____

_____

ACTION ITEMS:

_____

_____

_____

_____

_____

_____

SECTION IV

POSITIONING YOUR FIRM

◆

"Everything you do is marketing."

William Fay
Public Works Director

145

CHAPTER 14

POSITIONING FOR SELECTION SUCCESS

As you have learned in this book, there are a number of factors that can influence Selection Success. It can result from preparing a comprehensive and organized SOQ, giving a dynamic presentation and being technically capable of doing the job.

However, before a selection process even begins, there are a variety of ways that you can increase an owner's comfort level with your firm that can better position yourself for consideration on a future project. Below are some suggestions to consider.

1. **Volunteer to serve on selection panels if possible.** Check with the owner's selection coordinator to see if their organization allows outside representatives to sit on their panels. There may be legislative requirements, or some owners/agencies have internal procedures that provide for outside representatives, such as:

- Citizen representative.

- Professional architect, engineer or contractor.

- Facility user representative (i.e. museum board member or "Friends of the Library" representative).

Serving on these panels can provide a variety of benefits both to the owner and to your firm. It will allow you to:

- Enhance relationships by working side-by-side with the client.

- Possibly provide a service to the owner by meeting a legislative requirement.

- Display your knowledge and insight on project issues.

- Act as a trusted advisor to the owner.

- Experience a selection from the owner's point of view.

- Better understand what kind of issues matter most to this owner and how they make their selection decisions.

- Learn from other SOQs and interviews.

If this is an option, let the owner know that you are interested in serving as a selection panel member.

2. **Do the research.** The time to research a project is not after it has been advertised. Learn about upcoming projects by:

    - Talking to the client's project managers.

    - Reviewing public sector budgets.

    - Seeing if you can get on the mailing list for private sector business quarterly newsletters.

    - Reading business publications.

3. **Stay connected with your clients.** Talk to your client contacts on a regular basis and find opportunities to strengthen the relationship. Offer to be a resource for questions that might arise throughout the year.

4. **Provide excellent quality and service on projects you have already won.** Your best marketing tool is the project you already have. Owners want to work with people they can count on to do the job right. Whether you are the prime or a sub, your goal should be to exceed their expectations on your current work. A favorable (or unfavorable) past experience speaks louder than the most well-crafted SOQ or engaging interview.

5. **Handle disputes very well.** In all likelihood, you and your client will not agree on everything during the course of a project. We know that the adage that "The

client is always right" is not necessarily true. However, being a good partner to the client means being a team player, reasonable, committed, and willing to look at the situation from the client's perspective. It also means going the extra mile to preserve the relationship and providing quality customer service. And if there is a serious disagreement on a project, you should be committed to solving that disagreement as fairly and expeditiously as possible. You don't want to win a battle at the cost of losing a client.

6. **Stay active with professional associations and networking opportunities with potential clients.** The American Public Works Association (APWA) and the U. S. Green Building Council are examples of organizations composed of owners, consultants, and contractors. These organizations, and others like them, provide opportunities to:

- Chat one-on-one with client representatives in a more social atmosphere which allows them to know you on a more personal basis.

- Interact with other firms that provide different services which may result in new information or opportunities to collaborate on future projects.

- Become involved in various committees within the organization which promotes visibility and credibility, and helps your firm be perceived as a leader within your industry

As you see from the suggestions in this book, there are a number of things that firms can do to influence or impact their ability to get selected in a qualifications-based selection process.

Following the guidelines included in this book will increase your chances of Selection Success!

<u>NOTES</u>

KEY IDEAS IN THIS CHAPTER:

_____

_____

_____

_____

_____

_____

ACTION ITEMS:

_____

_____

_____

_____

_____

_____

THE AUTHORS

LORI STANLEY
HILARI WEINSTEIN

◆

*"People don't want to be 'marketed TO',
they want to be 'communicated WITH'."*

Flint McGlaughlin

Lori Stanley
Principal, Selection Solutions Consulting

Lori is an expert in managing selection and contracting processes for architects, engineers, consultants, construction managers at risk and design-builders.

She was responsible for managing the advertisement, selection, negotiation, and contract preparation for over a thousand qualification-based selection (QBS) processes during her 18 years as a Contracts Officer / Contracts Administration Supervisor for the City of Phoenix. These projects included parks, waterlines, streets, fire stations, and libraries. Lori also managed the consultant and/or Construction Manager at Risk selection processes for most of the City's largest projects, including runways, libraries, museums, and treatment plants, including the $500 million convention center expansion and the $1 billion Automated Train.

In 2006, Lori retired from the City and created Selection Solutions Consulting, Inc.. Lori works with consultants and contractors to help make their Statements of Qualifications and interview processes more effective. She also assists public owners in creating or improving their consultant, CM@Risk, and Design/Build QBS selection processes.

Lori has been an active member of the American Public Works Association (APWA) including eight years as a Director on the Board for the APWA Arizona Chapter. She has also been awarded emeritus status from the Alliance of Construction Excellence. Lori earned a Bachelor of Science in Business Management from Arizona State University.

Hilari Weinstein
President, High Impact Communication
Presentation Coaching Specialist

Hilari Weinstein knows what it takes to stand out against tough competition.   Out of thousands of collegiate competitors nationwide, she won two National Championship Titles at the American Forensics Association's Annual Collegiate Speaking Tournament.   In her first year as a coach, two of her students placed in the top five.

Her presentation coaching skills are sought after. Armed with a Master's degree in Speech Communication from The University of Texas at Austin (one of the top ranked communication schools in the country) and training from Coach University, in addition to years of experience in sales and sales training, Hilari has worked with clients nationwide to help make their presentations more effective and engaging.

Through customized workshops, interview preparation consulting and one-on-one coaching, her clients have gained greater confidence, effectiveness and influence *and* in the past few years alone, have secured numerous A/E/C projects valued at hundreds of millions of dollars.

In addition to serving on the faculty of the American Council of Engineering Companies (ACEC) Leadership Program, she is a regular columnist for Southwest Contractor Magazine and has been published in the Phoenix Business Journal. Currently, she is on the Board of Directors for the National Speakers Association, Arizona Chapter.

Contact Information

Lori Stanley
(623) 552-3858
www.selectionsolutionsgroup.com
lori@selectionsolutionsgroup.com

Hilari Weinstein
(602) 795-5400
www.highimpactcommunication.com
hilari@highimpactcommunication.com

For additional tools to help
your Selection Success,
go to our website at:
www.selectionsucess.com

Printed in the United States
130467LV00001B